Top row, left to right: (Karl Elieff), Marcel Dionne, Bobby Clarke, Don Awrey, Brian Glennie, Rod Seiling, Guy Lapointe, Richard Martin, Jean-Paul Parise, (Tommy Nayler).

Third row, left to right: (Joe Sgro), Yvan Cournoyer, Gary Bergman, Dale Tallon, Bill White, Peter Mahovlich, Serge Savard, Jocelyn Guevremont, Gilbert Perreault, Pat Stapleton, (John Forristall).

Second row, left to right: (Bob Haggert), Dennis Hull, Mickey Redmond, Paul Henderson, Gordon "Red" Berenson, Wayne Cashman, Vic Hadfield, Ed Johnston, Bill Goldsworthy, Ron Ellis, Rod Gilbert, (Mike Cannon).

Bottom row, left to right: Tony Esposito, Brad Park, Stan Mikita, Phil Esposito, (Harry Sinden, Alan Eagleson, John Ferguson), Frank Mahovlich, Jean Ratelle, Bobby Orr, Ken Dryden.

TEAM CANADA 1972

WHERE ARE THEY NOW?

BRIAN McFARLANE

WINDING STAIR PRESS

Text copyright © 2001 by Brian McFarlane

Special thanks to Ficel Marketing Corp.

National Library of Canada Cataloguing in Publication Data

McFarlane, Brian, 1931–

    Team Canada 1972 : where are they now?

ISBN 1-55366-086-2

1. Hockey players – Canada – Biography. 2. Hockey players – Soviet Union – Biography. 3. Canada-U.S.S.R. Hockey Series, 1972. I. Title.

GV848.5.A1M27 2001   796.962'092'2   C2001-903501-2

Winding Stair Press
An imprint of Stewart House Publishing Inc.
Etobicoke, Ontario
www.stewarthousepub.com
Executive Vice President and Publisher: Ken Proctor
Director of Publishing and Product Acquisition: Joe March

10 9 8 7 6 5 4 3 2 1
10 09 08 07 06 05 04 03 02 01

Jacket design by Darrin Laframboise
Book design by Counterpunch / Linda Gustafson

This book is available at special discounts for bulk purchases by groups or organizations for sales promotions, premiums, fundraising and educational purposes. For details, contact: Peter March, Stewart House Publishing Inc., Special Sales Department, 195 Allstate Parkway, Markham, Ontario. Tel: (866) 474-3478.

Printed and bound in Canada

PHOTO CREDITS

© Denis Brodeur

Pages: 8 (center); 16; 17; 20; 25; 26; 28 (background & inset); 30–31 (top); 30 (bottom, all); 31 (bottom, center & right); 32; 33 (background & inset); 36; 37 (top); 40; 41; 42; 43 (top); 45; 47; 49 (top & center); 52; 53; 54; 58 (top & bottom); 59; 60; 62 (background & inset); 63 (top & bottom); 64–65 (top); 64 (bottom, all); 65 (bottom, center & right); 67 (background & inset); 70; 71 (top & bottom); 72; 75; 76; 78; 80; 83; 85; 86; 89; 92; 94; 96 (background & inset); 97 (background & inset); 98 (bottom, center); 99 (bottom, left & center); 100 (inset); 101 (background & inset); 104; 105; 106; 108; 111; 112; 113; 116; 117; 121 (top & center); 122 (background); 124–125 (top); 124 (bottom, left & right); 125 (bottom, left & center); 126; 127 (background & inset); 132; 133; 135; 136; 141; 143; 145; 147; 148; 149; 151; 153; 155; 156 (top); 157; 158 (top); 161 (top & center); 162–167 (all); 169; 171; 174 (top); 175; 176; 177 (top); 179; 181; 184; 190 (top & bottom); 191.

© Bruce Bennett Studios, Farmingdale, NY

Pages: 23; 29; 31 (bottom, left); 35; 39; 48; 49 (bottom); 50 (top); 56; 57; 65 (bottom, left); 66; 69; 73 (bottom); 82; 98–99 (top); 98 (bottom, left & right); 99 (bottom, right); 100 (background); 103; 107; 119; 120; 122 (inset); 123; 124 (bottom, center); 125 (bottom, right); 128–129; 131; 139; 140; 150; 154; 158 (bottom); 160; 161 (bottom); 170; 172; 173; 183; 186; 189; 192 (top).

© Charles Kochman, System 4 Productions Inc., Downsview, ON

Pages: 14; 18; 21; 22; 27; 37 (bottom); 43 (bottom); 44; 50 (bottom); 55; 61; 73 (top); 76 (bottom); 81; 84; 90; 95; 109; 114; 115; 121 (bottom); 137; 138; 142; 146; 152; 156 (bottom); 159; 174 (bottom); 177 (bottom); 180; 185; 187; 192 (bottom).

Courtesy of The Hockey Hall of Fame
Page 3.

CONTENTS

INTRODUCTION

"Henderson! Henderson scores for Canada!"

In all of Canadian history, have any other spoken words become more famous? They were uttered three decades ago by Foster Hewitt, the nation's voice of hockey for half a century, and they triggered a nationwide celebration, unrestrained hysteria that almost rivaled the joy and sense of relief felt by millions on V-E Day, the day World War II ended.

Paul Henderson's goal on September 28, 1972, with just 34 seconds left on the clock in Moscow's Luzhniki Sports Palace, ended a month-long, eight-game series between the best players in the Soviet Union and a select team of NHL all-stars — Team Canada.

It was supposed to be a walkover, a rout for the Harry Sinden-coached NHLers. At last, the smug Soviets, winners of countless world titles in international hockey, would get their comeuppance against real players. The long-awaited series matched the best of the NHL pros versus the best amateurs on the globe and the pros were the overwhelming favorites.

Canada had dropped out of international hockey in 1970 because Canadian teams were denied the use of the nation's best players, the pros. And fourth-rate amateur teams just weren't good enough to win anymore, either at the world or Olympic championships.

When the announcement came — on April 20, 1972 — that an eight-game exhibition series between Team Canada and the Soviet all-stars would be played in September of that year, the idea was not universally endorsed.

The three NHL clubs in Canada at the time — Toronto, Montreal and Vancouver — immediately pledged their support for Hockey Canada, which organized the unique Summit Series. But initially there were howls of protest from some NHL clubs based in U.S. cities.

Boston Bruins President Weston Adams was the most vocal. "The entire idea is cock-eyed," he fumed. "I know I won't send any of my players to a Canadian team. Can you imagine us sending Bobby Orr and Phil Esposito and having them come back with a bad knee or a broken leg? There goes our season."

Adams and other governors were quietly and quickly pacified when they were reminded that a share of profits from the series would go toward the NHL Players' Association pension plan. It was money — a lot of money — the owners would have to cough up if the series was not sanctioned by all NHL teams.

Besides, the pros from the NHL would give the Soviets a good pasting and then come home. The series was no big deal.

As for Adams, he needn't have been concerned about Orr's participation. Following the Stanley Cup victory by the Bruins in '72, Orr required knee surgery and announced from his hospital bed that, "I would love to play against the Russians but I will not be ready physically to do so."

Derek Sanderson, one of Adams' hired guns, enthusiastically welcomed the idea, ignoring the disapproving comments from his boss. "I'm ready to be included. Any time, anywhere, count me in," he said. But Sanderson would flee to the rival World Hockey Association (WHA) in the off season, to become hockey's wealthiest player, and, like Bobby Hull who followed him to the upstart league, would therefore become ineligible to compete.

Former Montreal captain Jean Beliveau said, "I wish this breakthrough had come earlier. I would have loved to be on a team that faced the best of the Soviets."

Initially, Chicago's star left winger Bobby Hull issued a blunt refusal to become involved. In April, he told the *Hockey News*, "Count me out. The schedule is too long already without adding a high-pressure series in September." Hull later changed his tune, and his failure to earn a berth on Team Canada became political. He was banned because he'd fled the NHL for a 10-year, 2.75 million-dollar contract with the Winnipeg Jets of the WHA.

Millions of Hull fans railed at his exclusion, pointing to his spectacular record. By the end of the 1971–72 season, the Golden Jet had scored 604 goals, second only to Gordie Howe, and he'd been named to 12 all-star teams.

Brother Dennis Hull said, "Bobby's departure was devastating to the Blackhawks and to the league. Some of my Chicago teammates got together and offered to take less in salary if it meant we could keep Bobby in Chicago. We were naïve to think the Hawks didn't have enough cash to sign him. When he was shunned by Team Canada I offered to give up my position on the team in protest. But Bobby talked me out of it, saying it might turn out to be the 'chance of a lifetime.' It was certainly all of that."

Bobby Hull's renowned gift of gab may have been the biggest factor to cost him a spot on Team Canada. Initially, he was the first player named by the selection committee when they met in secret. Previously, NHL President Clarence Campbell, who was quite negative about the series, stated that "only players with NHL contracts could be on the team." Hull still had a signed contract with Chicago, even though he was headed for the WHA, so technically he was eligible. Hull was invited, agreed to play and was sworn to secrecy.

But the Golden Jet, during a sports dinner in the Maritimes, ignored the secrecy pact and blurted out that he would be joining Team Canada. When Campbell heard about Hull's comment, he called

the NHL governors and reminded them that, if Hull played, contracts of players named to the team would no longer be guaranteed by the NHL clubs in case of injury.

This was a major blow to Sinden and assistant coach John Ferguson. It was either purchase expensive insurance to guarantee contracts or drop Hull from the roster. They chose the latter, leaving Hull to say, "The biggest disappointment in my life was not being able to represent Canada in that famous 1972 series. I knew the Russians were good. I recall saying at the time that they had a pretty good chance at winning. All those reports that they couldn't skate, they had rotten goaltending — I knew that was all a bunch of malarkey."

Orr didn't agree. Prior to game one at the Montreal Forum, I sat next to Orr while he watched the Soviet players get through a pre-game skate. "Look!" he nudged me. "Look at how far they move in on the goalie before shooting. Our goaltenders would kill us if we did that." After watching the Soviets, wearing shabby equipment and skates, work out for an hour, Bobby didn't seem to think Team Canada had much to worry about.

Orr and Hull would have made Team Canada a much more powerful club had they played. Orr, winner of a second Conn Smythe Trophy as playoff MVP in 1972, joined Team Canada and traveled with them, and even skated with them for a few minutes one day, but was unable to perform. How much would Orr have strengthened Team Canada?

In six previous NHL seasons, he had won the Norris Trophy as the NHL's top defenseman five consecutive times and the Hart Trophy as MVP for the third consecutive year. He had scored 37 goals in each of the past two seasons and 33 the year before. He had led all individual scorers in 1970, an amazing feat for a defenseman and one he would duplicate in 1975.

Bobby Orr at practice with Ken Dryden in Moscow.

When the series opened in Montreal on September 2, nobody anticipated a Soviet victory, especially after Team Canada jumped into an early 2–0 lead. In a poll of experts conducted by the *Hockey News*, not one gave the Russians a chance. Not in the opening game, not in any game.

Fans even sympathized with 20-year-old Soviet goaltender Vladislav Tretiak, a newlywed who had been labeled a sieve by scouts who'd seen him

play (and seen him give up nine goals) on the day following his wedding.

Former Canadiens' star goalie Jacques Plante took Tretiak aside when he arrived in Montreal and gave him a few tips on how to play the NHL forwards. "I was thinking of the humiliation he was almost certain to suffer," explained Plante. But there would be no humiliation – only honor – for the soft-spoken young Russian.

In game one, Tretiak would embark on a journey that would take him to the Hockey Hall of Fame in 1989, the first Soviet player to be so honored.

"I knew we were facing a very strong team," he said. "One that was well liked by the fans. The fact that I, a 20-year-old boy, was going to play against them was almost overwhelming."

After giving up those two early goals in the series' first few minutes, Tretiak settled down and outshone Dryden, the premier goaltender of that era. Tretiak's teammates, displaying great speed and tenacity, battled back to tie the score in the first, added two more goals by dynamic Valeri Kharlamov in the second and put three more past Dryden in the third. Final score: Soviets 7, Team Canada 3. It was an unbelievable upset. Across Canada, millions of hockey fans watched their TV screens in consternation, wide-eyed and open-mouthed. In Team Canada's dressing room, defenseman Brad Park put it succinctly: "Holy shit, were we shocked." Ken Dryden added, "It

was awful, really awful. I felt like a fish on land during that game."

What had the advance scouts been thinking when they returned from their mission with a declaration that all was well? There were few players of NHL caliber in all of the Soviet Union, they affirmed, and the young Soviet goaltender – a kid named Tretiak – was padded, porous and pathetic.

"We were dyin' after the first period of that first game," Phil Esposito recalled. "We were walkin' around the dressing room sayin', 'It's hot. It's so friggin' hot!' Well, it was hot all right in the building. But we were suffering."

"I remember how strong they were," said Yvan Cournoyer. "I couldn't believe their strength and conditioning. And some of them were not much bigger than me."

"Did we ever get fooled," Ferguson said after game one. "I remember thinking the shock waves would be felt all over the world."

"This team we met from Russia wasn't an amateur team," said Boston Bruin enforcer Wayne Cashman. "No way. They were more professional than we were. And they were ready."

Defenseman Serge Savard added, "Those guys were not staying with their families. They trained 12 months of the year while we trained for three weeks."

Goalie Ken Dryden philosophized, "You don't underestimate your opponent. You never underestimate your opponent."

But it was obvious that everyone had underestimated the young Soviet stars.

At the final buzzer, Team Canada players skated off, dazed and bewildered. They either forgot or decided to ignore the anticipated post-game handshakes with their victors and were branded poor losers by a hostile media.

"We got beat by one fine hockey team," coach Sinden admitted at a post-game press conference.

Winger Dennis Hull, a spectator that night, entered the dressing room and saw players looking helpless. Others looked distraught, as if they might begin to cry.

"Game two became critical," said Ron Ellis.

Team Canada bounced back to capture game two in Toronto's Maple Leaf Gardens by a 4−1 score. Few who witnessed it will ever forget a masterful goal by Peter Mahovlich, who, while killing a penalty, treated first a Russian defender and then Tretiak to a "now you see it, now you don't" routine that ended in a goal and a standing ovation.

Game three in Winnipeg ended in a 4−4 tie and game four in Vancouver saw the Soviets win 5−3 and the NHLers booed off the ice. The disenchantment began early in Vancouver, after Bill Goldsworthy recklessly earned not one but two minor penalties. And the Soviets' Boris Mikhailov sent Canadian hopes spinning with a pair of power play goals while Goldsworthy squirmed in the penalty box. After that, Team Canada was forced to open up and the Soviets began smacking their lips. "They'll eat you for lunch when you open things up," said Paul Henderson, shaking his head. Seconds after the game, Phil Esposito, drenched in sweat, delivered an emotional speech. He admitted the Soviets had a great team but he was appalled to be booed by his fellow Canadians.

"To the people across Canada, we tried. We gave it our best. To the people who booed us, geez, all of us guys are really disheartened. We're disillusioned and disappointed. We cannot believe the bad press that we've got, the booing we've got in our own building.

"I'm completely disappointed. I cannot believe it. Every one of us guys − 35 guys − we came out because we love our country. Not for any other reason. We came because we love Canada."

Phil skated off toward the dressing room and a leather lung in the stands immediately blistered him with criticism. Phil said, "I was so mad I felt like ramming my stick right down his throat. That's when I realized we were in a war, man. This isn't a game. This is a war and we'd better get ourselves together."

Team Canada did get its act together. Phil's rant registered. Everyone talked about it. It would become a turning point in the series.

With the conclusion of the four-game Canadian segment of the 1972 series, North American fans, especially those living in Canada, felt that the damage to NHL prestige was crushing. The Soviet

skaters, wearing shabby skates and using well-worn sticks, had scored 17 goals in the first four games.

To long-time followers of NHL hockey, this was incredible, a stunning surprise. They searched for reasons for the debacle. They blamed overly optimistic journalists and broadcasters. Team Canada members were treated to a barrage of advance publicity proclaiming their invincibility. What team would not succumb to overconfidence? What team would not believe press clippings that heralded it "the best ever assembled"?

With a two-week breather before the games resumed in Moscow, North Americans began to wonder if the series was such a grand idea after all. There was a lot of national pride and prestige at stake, and the Soviets, already holding an edge, now held the added advantage of home ice for the remainder of the series.

Perhaps Weston Adams, president of the Boston Bruins, who thought the NHL was making a huge mistake in approving the series, had been on the mark after all.

Two rough exhibition games on the large European-size ice in Stockholm, Sweden, helped bring Team Canada closer together, even though the Swedish fans heaped scorn on them for their stick work and bruising bodychecks. But it was a Team Canada player, Wayne Cashman, who took the dirtiest foul, a stick in the mouth that caused a horrible wound.

What might be called a minor mutiny took place when the team reached Moscow. Veteran player Vic Hadfield ("I scored 50 goals, Harry, and I can't get on the ice. I'm better than Parise") and youngsters Jocelyn Guevremont, Richard Martin and Gilbert Perreault quit the team and returned to Canada.

Team Canada fell deeper into the hockey pit when they blew a 4–1 lead in game five, and lost 5–4. Paul Henderson scored two of Team Canada's goals. "I let the team down," Tony Esposito said afterward. "I stopped everything for two periods, then gave up four goals in just over five minutes. I can't believe I did that."

"Don't worry, Tony," Rod Gilbert said. "We're a team now. We all know it. I say we're going to win the next three games."

A huge ovation from the 3,200 Canadian fans in the arena boosted the players' spirits and they squeezed out a 3–2 victory in game six. During the game, assistant coach John Ferguson called Bobby Clarke over to the boards. He pointed at Soviet star Valeri Kharlamov: "Bobby, this guy is killin' us. Do something! Break his ankle. Anything. Get him out of there!"

Clarke got the message.

"He (Kharlamov) gave me a little dig with his stick, then turned and took off. I went after him and gave him quite a whack across the ankle. At the time it seemed like a good thing to do. Later,

maybe it seemed like a bad thing to do. But I was never ashamed of doing it."

The injury put Kharlamov out of the game. He returned for game eight, his luster considerably dimmed.

Harry Sinden was livid over the officiating in game six. Team Canada players served 31 penalty minutes, the Soviets a mere 4.

In game seven, the teams were locked in a 4—4 tie late in the contest. Then, at 17:54 of the third period, Henderson scored a dramatic goal that turned out to be the game-winner.

Interest was at a peak for game eight. Across Canada, school classes gathered in gymnasiums, where TV sets were installed. Shops closed, workers called in "sick" and every TV set and radio in the nation was turned on with the volume up high.

Team Canada was hit with two early penalties and the Soviets edged in front on a power play goal.

When Jean-Paul Parise was penalized for interference, he tore after referee Josef Kompalla and threatened to decapitate the frightened official with his stick. Parise was tossed out of the game.

At the end of two periods, the Soviets led 5—3 and hopes for a Canadian triumph plummeted. But Team Canada came flying back in the third. Esposito scored, then Cournoyer rapped in a rebound. When the red light failed to flicker, Canadian players and fans went wild. Al Eagleson created such a commotion at rinkside, he was manhandled by

Russian soldiers. Pete Mahovlich, his stick held high, led a charge to the boards and rescued Eagleson, pulling him onto the ice. As he was led to the comparative safety of the Team Canada bench, Eagleson gave the Soviets a memorable one-finger salute. The goal judge turned out to be Viktor Dombrowski, a Soviet referee whose slow trigger finger made him public enemy number one in the Canadian camp. Dombrowski would shrug and say, "Light switch broken. Not work."

With the score tied and time running out, word reached the Team Canada bench that the Soviets would claim victory because of the one goal margin they held over the eight games played.

In the final minute, Paul Henderson stood at the bench and barked at Pete Mahovlich, "Get off the ice. I'm coming on."

He flew into the Soviet zone and failed to control a pass from Cournoyer that went in front of him. Henderson fell into the boards behind Tretiak. Two Soviet defenders stumbled over the puck in the faceoff circle and Esposito reached in and stole it. He fired a shot that Tretiak turned aside. Henderson had regained his feet, moved in front and grabbed the rebound. He shot hard at Tretiak. No goal. Tretiak saved. There was another rebound. Henderson shot again. His second try was successful. The light went on as Tretiak sprawled. When asked years later how often he thought about that goal, Tretiak would say, "Every day of my life."

Team Canada '72 holding commemorative trophies during the induction of Team Canada '72 as Team of the Twentieth Century at the Hockey Hall of Fame in 2000. From left to right, front row: Jean-Paul Parise, Rod Gilbert, Yvan Cournoyer, Harry Sinden, Stan Mikita, Ron Ellis, Paul Henderson, Don Awrey. Second row: Vic Hadfield, Ed Johnston, Red Berenson, Pat Stapleton, Dennis Hull, Rod Seiling, Peter Mahovlich, a representative from the Canadian mint, Tony Esposito, Serge Savard, Jean Ratelle, Brian Glennie. Third row: Richard Martin, John Ferguson, Bill White, Jocelyn Guevremont, Ken Dryden. Not in attendance: Wayne Cashman, Bobby Clarke, Marcel Dionne, Phil Esposito, Guy Lapointe, Frank Mahovlich, Brad Park, Gilbert Perreault, Mickey Redmond, Dale Tallon. Deceased: Gary Bergman, Bill Goldsworthy.

Henderson, for a split second, thought of his father, Garnet Henderson, who died before the series began. "Oh, he'd have loved to see this sucker," was his thought.

"Henderson has scored for Canada," screamed Foster Hewitt into his microphone and unparalleled joy swept through the hearts of Canadians wherever they heard that triumphant shout.

The final few seconds of the game were played out and the celebrations began. What started as a series of exhibition games that would surely prove Canadian players were the best in the world ended on a note of high drama – a titanic struggle with the issue in doubt until the final moments.

Three decades have passed since Henderson leaped into the arms of Yvan Cournoyer to celebrate hockey's most famous goal, three decades since Pat Stapleton grabbed the puck and kept it, three decades since fans saluted Phil Esposito's leadership and the tenacity of the Clarke-Ellis-Henderson line, the last three players picked for the team, three decades since that astonishing comeback.

Where are they now, these heroes we at times vilified, then treasured, revered and adored in 1972? What memories can they share with us, what untold stories can they reveal of the greatest hockey series ever played?

DON AWREY

Don Awrey joined the Boston Bruins in 1963–64 and became a regular on defense for the 1965–66 season. He played seven seasons with the Bruins and was on Cup winning teams in 1970 and 1972. After two seasons in St. Louis he was traded to Montreal, where he played on another Cup winner.

The highlight in 1972 for me was simply to be invited to training camp. It surprised me. I mean, who knew that the series would turn out to be as exciting as it was? If it had gone the way our scouts thought it would, then Team Canada wouldn't have been the big deal it turned out to be.

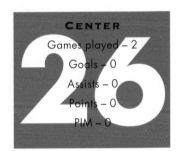

CENTER
Games played – 2
Goals – 0
Assists – 0
Points – 0
PIM – 0

26

They invited guys to camp promising certain things: everyone believed they were going to be playing two or three games each. You know we all wanted our ice time. Harry and Fergie were going to mold a team where we would all intermingle and there would be several different lineups. We all thought we would be playing in the same number of games. Because it was going to be a walkover, right? Everybody told us that. From the first day of training camp, according to the scouts, we were supposed to win all eight games. And we were told that Tretiak was not a good goaltender, a real amateur, and their team just wasn't on a par with ours. But as we all know it worked out quite a bit different than that.

Some guys were a little unhappy with the treatment they received. Me? I was just happy to be there because I knew I wasn't one of the top defensemen in the NHL at that time. I never expected to be invited. But it turned out that Orr was hurt and a few other guys couldn't go, and they went down the list until they came to me. I heard later that Sinden wanted me but Fergie didn't.

I played two games in the series.

I played the first game, which I deserved to start because Rod Seiling and I played very, very well in the training camp. Harry Sinden rewarded us both by allowing us that honor. The Rangers big line of Gilbert-Ratelle-Hadfield played that night too, and I remember Gilbert saying, "Geez, I wanted to score so badly and I played two shifts without even touching the puck. The Russians wouldn't let us have it."

So we lost the opener and everybody in the lineup had to take some blame for that. Remember, just because you put 30 or 35 people together and put the same uniforms on them, that does not make them a team. The Russians were a team because they had been practicing hard and working together as a unit for a year prior to the series. They were a team and we were not. We did not become a team until later on in the series.

In that first game in Montreal, Ken Dryden was in goal. Over the years, and I'm sure Ken will agree with this, for some reason Ken had not been

Awrey, center, fending off Boris Mikhailov at the Canadian net in Montreal. The other Team Canada players are Brad Park, Ken Dryden, Mickey Redmond and Paul Henderson.

I thought Don Awrey was a good competitor. He was a good, hard player and solid NHLer. I came down on him many, many nights and while we respected each other greatly, we didn't really enjoy playing against each other. I remember that first practice, I skated up beside him and I said, "Don, it's kind of nice to be on the same team for a change." – *Ron Ellis*

known to play his best hockey against international competition. I know what kind of goaltender he is because I was a teammate of his with the Canadiens and then I played against him for many years. But he was not in his best form in Montreal that night. In hindsight, perhaps he shouldn't have started. Perhaps Rod Seiling and I shouldn't have played in that first game, either. I know I was

blamed for one Russian goal, scored by a guy who supposedly walked around me, skating on my outside. To me that was not a very good goal, even though he might have gotten me by half a stride. But that goal opened the game up.

I also played in Vancouver, which was another loss, a real disaster. The whole country kind of came down on us in Vancouver. But you must remember, two power play goals were scored on us when Billy Goldsworthy, God bless him, took two penalties early in the first period. If you take those goals away, then the 5–3 score doesn't look so bad. We were a little better represented than the score of that game might indicate.

After that game, when I heard Phil Esposito's speech, that's when he instantly became the leader of Team Canada. When he stood up for us and said that we were trying our best, and that there was a lot of pressure on us, I was really impressed. We couldn't believe we were in such an ugly position after four games, with a single win, two losses and a tie.

The two low moments were in Vancouver and Montreal. Everybody agrees on that. Then we regrouped in Sweden. Wayne Cashman and I had some testy moments with the Swedes, and I think we were taking out all our frustrations on our opponents, which was really unfair to them. Cashman said something like, "Where were you guys in World War II?" And it got in the papers over there. Later, Cash was speared in the mouth by a Swede and took about 30 stitches in his tongue.

The Canadian consulate in Sweden did not defend us or give us much help because I guess we played like Canadians have always played. And of course the Swedes, with their bigger ice surface, were not used to playing the Canadian-style of game.

When we got to Moscow, I did not play in any of those games. I was a cheerleader from the stands and was very much behind my teammates. We had our ups and downs, but we practiced every day with the idea that we were going to have to make a comeback. And we never lost our faith. I was glad that I stayed and became a part of history even though I didn't get to play in those games. I'm still very proud to be remembered as part of that club.

When Vic Hadfield said he was ready to go home, and he, along with a few other young players, left, I understood his situation. Vic had just enjoyed a great year with the New York Rangers, he had just signed a new contract and it was obvious Harry was not going to play him against the Russians. So he thought he owed it to the Rangers to come back and go right to the New York training camp.

Awrey, center, blocks Vladimir Vikulov as Frank Mahovlich moves in for the puck.

I don't think Vic and the others were considered deserters or quitters. I would have gone to bat for any one of them who left. I think they left because they thought that they were doing the right thing, and had the best interests of their teams in mind. I think the fans and the writers at the time were wrong to put any blame on them because the fans did not know the whole story and the writers did

Don Awrey at the Hockey Hall of Fame, 2000.

not write the whole story. They wrote that Hadfield and the others were leaving a sinking ship. It wasn't that way at all.

One of the guys on Team Canada who really impressed me was Phil Esposito. I always knew what he could do, but I really have to admire how he became our leader. Even though I didn't play with him that much during the series, he made me realize what a great leader he was.

They invited guys to camp promising certain things: everyone believed they were going to be playing two or three games each. You know we all wanted our ice time. Because it was going to be a walkover, right? Everybody told us that. From the first day of training camp, according to the scouts, we were supposed to win all eight games.

For the Russians, Kharlamov was their brightest star. He was fast, so hard to defend against out there. I admired the way he used to come from behind and how he kept everyone on their toes. He was simply outstanding. You had to be very careful not to take a run at him — chances are he'd be gone when you got there. The Russian team in general, especially their forwards, were so good with their feet, with their sticks and all their sharp little passes. They really impressed me.

Bobby Orr could not play in that series, but oh, how he wanted to. He was with us from start to finish. Had his knees been healthy, I think he would have made the difference in us not having to play the last game, or the last two games, for the win. I think he would have turned game one around for us, or game three at some point, or even game four. Bobby Orr would have made a huge difference. We would have been in a much better position if he had played.

I found it very difficult, when I came back to the NHL, to play against my Team Canada teammates when they were on the opposing team. I just couldn't go against them the way I wanted to, the way I should have. It was hard to play aggressively against them, to be very physical with them, because they had become my lifelong friends.

Since 1972, I have kept myself busy with a variety of different ventures. I owned a pub/restaurant in the Boston area and went on to be a sports representative selling equipment. I also took tours from the Boston area up to Montreal to see the Canadiens play. Currently I am retired and spend eight months of the year in Naples, Florida. I still find time to go on the ice twice a week and feel quite comfortable out there, even at my advanced age.

GORDON "RED" BERENSON

Gordon "Red" Berenson was the first Canadian player to jump directly to the NHL from U.S. college hockey, joining the Montreal Canadiens in 1961–62 from the University of Michigan. Berenson was traded to the New York Rangers in 1966 but did not become an NHL star until he joined the St. Louis Blues in 1968–69. He remains the only NHL player to score six goals in a road game. He was traded to Detroit on February 6, 1971, and returned to the Blues on December 30, 1974. He scored 261 goals in 987 games. Currently, he is the revered head coach at Michigan. In 2001 his team played Michigan State to a 3–3 tie before a record outdoor crowd of 74,554 at Spartan Stadium in East Lansing.

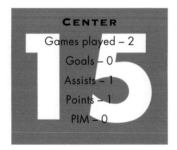

CENTER

Games played – 2

Goals – 0

Assists – 1

Points – 1

PIM – 0

15

I suppose I was one of a small number of players on Team Canada '72 who had ever faced the Russians. In 1959, while attending the University of Michigan on a hockey scholarship, I was invited to play for the Belleville McFarlands in the world championships, and our team defeated the Russians to win the championship.

I think the best part of the series was the excitement leading up to the first game. Obviously, that was a hugely anticipated moment. I remember the electricity in the Montreal Forum before the game as the puck dropped. It was a special hockey game and a special tournament to be having NHL players play against the Russians, so there was a ton of excitement. And it went from the best to the worst. An hour and a half later, when our team realized that we were being outclassed in that game, I think that all of Canada was shocked, just as the players and the media were. Everyone was shocked. So that was the start of the tournament, but I think we had the run of emotions right from the peak to the pits in the very first game.

I think it was a wonderful tribute to us that Canada rallied behind this team even though there were some real question marks and a lot of second-guessing going on as we fell behind in the series. We came together in that eighth game, we created a moment that millions of Canadians will remember for the rest of their lives. I think it was great for the country.

Our knowledge of the Russian players was very limited. We didn't know one from the other when we first started the series. From the players' standpoint, we didn't have a lot of information. I know they sent a scouting contingent over to Russia to see those players play, but I don't think that we had a great scouting report on that team. I don't

I remember the electricity in the Montreal Forum before the game as the puck dropped. It was a special hockey game and a special tournament to be having NHL players play against the Russians, so there was a ton of excitement. And it went from the best to the worst.

Berenson and Aleksandr Maltsev fight for possession of the puck.

know if it would have even been possible to get one. Going over to Russia – it's enough trouble just finding your way around and getting to the rink, let alone identifying players, especially if they knew you were there. They might have changed numbers and done whatever they wanted to do to throw you off balance.

The experience in Russia made me appreciate how fortunate we are to live in a free country – I can't say enough about that. I came back to Detroit on one of the fans' airplanes. When the captain announced that we had flown over the Iron Curtain, people started crying and cheering and singing "O Canada" – it was unbelievable! Just to get out of the country!

As a result, we did not have the respect for their skills or their conditioning that we needed to have. But everyone was really impressed with Kharlamov – he was an extremely fast, skilled player. And we all came to respect Tretiak and Yakushev as being solid, even NHL-type, players.

On our team, there is no question that Esposito asserted himself, and probably played the best hockey of his career. He was already an established player, but to play the way he did and to lead the way he did in that series was really impressive from a teammate's standpoint. And Paul Henderson scoring clutch goals – it wasn't just the last game, it was the games before that, too, that he scored huge goals and was a real positive influence.

I think we were all disappointed in the players who left. That was hard to justify. Although we all understood the duress and frustration that they were going through, it wasn't something you wanted to walk away from at that point. I'm sure there are a lot of regrets among them still.

In terms of hockey, the series made me appreciate that North America doesn't have a monopoly on the sport. We gained an appreciation for some of the off-ice conditioning that the Europeans were doing and the continued development of skills that we see to this day with the European players. I know that has helped me in my coaching career.

The experience in Russia made me appreciate how fortunate we are to live in a free country – I can't say enough about that. There were a few of us who had to get back to our training camps – I didn't go to Czechoslovakia and I probably wasn't going to play there anyway – so I came back to Detroit on one of the fans' airplanes. When the captain announced that we had flown over the Iron Curtain, people started crying and cheering and singing "O Canada" – it was unbelievable! Just to get out of the country! We landed in Helsinki as a stop-off point to fuel up before flying the rest of the way. When we landed, it was the same thing – people had tears in their eyes. It was very emotional coming off that airplane, just knowing we were out of Russia.

I retired from the St. Louis Blues in '78 and became an assistant coach there. Then I was the head coach of the Blues for three years [Berenson won the Jack Adams Trophy as the NHL's coach of the year in 1981]. I ended up in Buffalo as an assistant coach for two years. My son was interested in attending the University of Michigan, so I drove him over to Ann Arbor one day and they recruited me to coach at Michigan. In June of '84, I came back to Ann Arbor and I've been here ever since. This will be my 18th year coaching college hockey. I really enjoy it because I've always been a big believer in education, and I took this route myself. I got my bachelor's and my master's degree at the University of Michigan. With the development of

Gordon "Red" Berenson.

college hockey – we've seen a lot of college players step into the NHL – it's nice for them to be able to do that with a degree in their pockets.

We've had some success here at Michigan. While I've been here, Brendan Morrison won the Hobey Baker Award and we've won two national championships. We've had a great run, so it's been a very fulfilling part of my hockey career.

GARY BERGMAN

Defenseman Gary Bergman, universally praised by his Team Canada teammates, his Soviet adversaries and thousands of fans across Canada for his sterling play in 1972, did not live to celebrate the 30th anniversary of the Summit Series. On December 8, 2000, Bergman passed away in Detroit after an eight-month battle with cancer. He was 62. Bergman, a Kenora, Ontario, native, spent four seasons in the minor leagues before joining the Detroit Red Wings in 1964–65. In his 10th season with Detroit he was traded to Minnesota. The following year (1974–75) he was traded back to the Red Wings. He retired in 1975–76 after spending one season with the Kansas City Scouts.

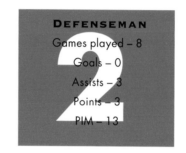

DEFENSEMAN
Games played – 8
Goals – 0
Assists – 3
Points – 3
PIM – 13

With Team Canada in '72, a team loaded with skilled, colorful defenders, Bergman quietly made his presence felt in training camp. He stood out on a roster loaded with top NHL stars: Park, Savard, Lapointe, White, Stapleton and others. At 33, he was older than most of his mates and neither as fast nor as flashy as most of them. But throughout the series, to the surprise of many observers, he was very effective and very consistent. He was called "gritty," "tenacious" and "a character player" by the media. Soviet forwards, noting his receding hairline, perhaps assumed he would not be able to cope with their speed and finesse. They were wrong. They soon found out he was just as difficult to outsmart as any of his more notable brethren guarding the Canadian blueline. Harry Sinden would say, "We got a marvelous series out of Gary Bergman. He was incredible. It was a bit of a surprise because he was a guy we picked for the team but we weren't really sure he'd be able to make it. If it was a bit of a gamble, it really paid off, for he was damn good on every shift."

In game seven in Moscow, Bergman caught everyone's attention by drilling Soviet centerman Boris Mikhailov into the boards late in the third period. It triggered a fight that emptied both benches. Watching on TV, Canadians were infuriated to see Mikhailov lash out at Bergman with his feet, kicking him on the shins and attempting to injure him with his flashing blades.

Gary Bergman signing memorabilia at the Royal York Hotel, Toronto, 1997.

I'd like to single out the late Gary Bergman as an unsung hero who produced a lot and surprised me. He probably played the best eight games of his life in the series and he was as steady as a rock on our defense. – *Harry Sinden*

Bergman in a race with Boris Mikhailov, Moscow.

Bergman had never been treated in such a dastardly manner in any of his many NHL games, in which kicking is a no-no, as rare as a slam-dunk or a touchdown. But he wasn't about to ignore Mikhailov's naughtiness. He dealt with his opponent by banging his head into the wire mesh atop the boards — hard and often.

"I couldn't believe the guy was actually kicking me," he would tell Bill White later. "If a bunch of guys hadn't intervened and pulled me away, I was ready to kill the s.o.b. It was just moments after that

when Paul Henderson came through with the winning goal. He rushed in alone on two Russian defenders and beat them both. He pushed the puck around one, then picked it up again and beat the next guy. Even though he was hit and knocked off balance, while falling he fired a shot under Tretiak's arm for what turned out to be the game-winner. Even though he scored a more famous one in game eight, that goal by Henderson assured us of a chance to win the series. It was a spectacular play and one of the most remarkable goals I ever saw."

WAYNE CASHMAN

Wayne Cashman, a veteran of 17 seasons with the Boston Bruins, played left wing for Phil Esposito and Ken Hodge, helping to form one of the NHL's most prolific lines in the 1970s. He played on Cup winners in Boston in 1970 and 1972. He was team captain of the Bruins from 1977–78 until his retirement in 1983. He's been a coach, assistant coach and scout in the NHL. He scored 277 goals and earned 793 points in 1,027 games.

I guess what threw everybody off before the series started were the scouting reports on the Russians. The two scouts we sent over there came back and said that scouting the Russians was a joke. They watched a game from a little press box and they had no programs or lineups. They didn't know who the players were on the ice and the goalie, Tretiak, looked awful. When Tretiak turned out to be so good against us, the scouts were embarrassed. But if he looked dreadful when they saw him over there, what were they supposed to say – that he was the reincarnation of Georges Vezina?

You know, Tretiak did look a bit shaky in the opening minutes of game one of the series, giving up two quick goals. But after that, the guy was terrific. And the guys in front of him were even better, with their effortless skating, great conditioning and their tricky passes. In winning 7–3,

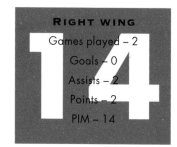

RIGHT WING

14

Games played – 2

Goals – 0

Assists – 2

Points – 2

PIM – 14

they made us look bad and they stunned a nation. Right after the opening faceoff, we go ahead 2–0 and we're laughing. It's going to be a one-sided series, right, like everybody predicted. Then bang, bang, bang, bang, they're ahead 4–2 and they bang in three more. Shit! We didn't know what hit us.

For game two, Harry Sinden decided he needed stronger forechecking and more physical play. So I got to play and so did Stan Mikita, Bill Goldsworthy, Peter Mahovlich and some others. I remember how deadly serious we were in the dressing room compared with the casual attitude that existed before game one. It was in that game that big Pete scored a goal that has to rate as one of the all-time best – a shorthanded goal that gave our team a huge lift and helped us tie the series with a 4–1 win. That made us feel better.

In Winnipeg, I got tossed by the referee midway through the third period after I took a couple of slashing penalties. Bobrov, the Russian coach, apparently told the referee I should have spent the entire game in the penalty box, and would have if the game were played in Europe. That was

When Tretiak turned out to be so good against us, the scouts were embarrassed. But if he looked dreadful when they saw him over there, what were they supposed to say – that he was the reincarnation of Georges Vezina?

Cashman is blocked by Vladimir Lutchenko and a flurry of Russians, while Phil Esposito sneaks around the net, Toronto.

a first. I hadn't heard anything like that before. The game ended in a tie, but Paul Henderson (who else?) almost won it for us with a shot in the third period. Tretiak made an outstanding save on Henny.

I didn't play in the Vancouver loss, which everybody agrees was the lowest point of the series for us. After that game, my Boston teammate, Phil Esposito, stood up and told the country exactly what he thought of them, and us, and everything involved. It was how we all felt. It was one of the most emotional moments of the entire series and it didn't even take place on the ice.

We played a pair of brutal, ugly games in Sweden and in one of them, Ulf Sterner, a 17-year veteran of Swedish hockey and a guy who once played four games with the New York Rangers, caught me

Right after the opening faceoff, we go ahead 2–0 and we're laughing. Then bang, bang, bang, bang, they're ahead 4–2 and they bang in three more. Shit! We didn't know what hit us.

right in the mouth with his stick, severely lacerating my tongue. That's as painful an injury as you can have. I didn't even see him when he came up from behind me and speared me. And it happened when the period was over. I never went back at him – never had a chance to.

Vic Hadfield took a lot of crap from Lars Erik Sjoberg in that game and finally he whacked him and broke his nose. The next day, the Swedish papers called us "gangsters" and played up Sjoberg's bent nose, but not a word about my bloody tongue.

In Winnipeg, I got tossed by the referee midway through the third period after I took a couple of slashing penalties. Bobrov, the Russian coach, apparently told the referee I should have spent the entire game in the penalty box, and would have if the game were played in Europe.

Cashman taking a slide into Tony Esposito's net; Evgeni Mishakov already heading off in the other direction.

Almost as painful as my mouth was the horrible refereeing we had to deal with in Moscow. Harry said the officiating in game six was the worst he had ever seen. It sure woke the players up to what we were all up against. Paul Henderson scored the winning goal in that game after we blew a lead and lost game five. After game six, we really felt we had the Russians on the ropes. We all had a

feeling that now we were headed up and they were going down. And when someone stole our beer that really pissed us off.

In game seven, Henny scored another winning goal – a beauty! He beat two Russian defenders to score on Tretiak. He told me he'd never done anything like it before, even in practice. That goal, and Pete Mahovlich's in Toronto, were two of the prettiest goals I'd ever seen.

Then there was all that political bullshit before game eight, when we were supposed to have Dahlberg and Bata as referees. It was our choice. But the Russians told us Dahlberg was sick even though he looked fine a few minutes earlier. What bull! We were stuck with Kompalla, a West German ref we all hated, and Bata, a Czech.

And when we trailed 5–3 after two periods, the Russians put a lot of extra water on the ice, I guess to slow us down for the first few minutes of the final period. But Harry countered by keeping us in the dressing room until the ice was firm. Harry and Fergie were always looking for little tricks they might have up their sleeve.

Then Espo scored early in the final period, which gave us a boost. Then Cournoyer scored. Finally Henderson popped up in front of Tretiak and scored the biggest goal of his life – some call it the biggest goal ever – and we'd won it. What a storybook ending! And what a great feeling! Even though I didn't get to play in the final game it was a super feeling. I've never seen so many tears shed in a dressing room – tears of joy.

On the trip home there was another huge celebration. People tell me I looked a little woozy when I got off the plane. I tell them it was from breathing that good, clean Canadian air once again.

There were guys on Team Canada who took their game to new heights in that series. A perfect example would be Bobby Clarke. After that series, he was recognized as a superstar in the NHL. And Guy Lapointe. I was so impressed with Guy because he was such a young player and he was huge in that series.

The '72 series wasn't such a big deal in the U.S., where some of us played on American teams, but it was huge in Canada. It affected the whole country and it brought Canadian fans a great deal of pride. Every Canadian youngster grew up thinking the NHL was still the best league in the world. His heroes had just proved it. And the guys on that team were my heroes, too. After all these years, I still have a great deal of respect for my teammates on that club.

Wayne Cashman coached the Tampa Bay Lightning in the late 1980s.

I've stayed with hockey in a coaching and scouting capacity since I retired from the NHL in 1983. I'm currently an assistant coach with my old club, the Boston Bruins, a team with which I spent 17 seasons and helped to win two Stanley Cups.

Just prior to the 2001–02 season, I lost a good friend in Ace Bailey when those terrorists flew the plane he was on into the World Trade Center in New York. I spent a couple of hours with Ace the night before his tragic death. We were in his home in Lynnfield, Massachusetts, and he kept telling his son, "Make sure you take care of your mom." He must have said it four or five times that night, as though he had a premonition or something like that.

CANADA

Game 1: September 2, 1972

Montreal Forum, Montreal

Heavily favored by both sides in the series, the Canadians scored first after only 30 seconds and then again six minutes later. The series was already in the bag.

However, this game was anything but in the bag. The Soviets scored at the 11:40 mark and then tied things up with a pretty, shorthanded goal.

The great Kharlamov introduced himself to Canadians from coast to coast, scoring twice in the second frame in impressive fashion.

Bobby Clarke, who would establish himself as a workhorse throughout the series, brought the Canadians to within a point at 8:32 in the third period. But three unanswered goals by the Soviets in the last five minutes made the final 7–3 and astonished the pundits.

Prior to the match, people such as coaching legend Punch Imlach had predicted the Canadians would win every game by five or six goals. Hall of Fame netminder Jacques Plante felt so badly for 20-year-old Vladislav Tretiak that he took time before game one to teach the youngster the shooting tendencies of the biggest threats Team Canada would put on the ice that night.

By the end of it all, the Canadians were so worried and winded that they skated off the ice without tending first to the traditional formality of the post-game handshake.

Stats

USSR 7, Canada 3
Attendance: 18,818.

FIRST PERIOD

1. Canada, P. Esposito (F. Mahovlich, Bergman) 0:30.
2. Canada, Henderson (Clarke) 6:32.
3. USSR, Zimin (Yakushev, Shadrin) 11:40.
4. USSR, Petrov (Mikhailov) 17:28.
Penalties: Henderson 1:03; Yakushev 7:04; Mikhailov 15:11; Ragulin 17:19.

SECOND PERIOD

5. USSR, Kharlamov (Maltsev) 2:40.
6. USSR, Kharlamov (Maltsev) 10:18.
Penalties: Clarke 5:16; Lapointe 12:53.

THIRD PERIOD

7. Canada, Clarke (Ellis, Henderson) 8:32.
8. USSR, Mikhailov (Blinov) 13:32.
9. USSR, Zimin (unassisted) 14:29.
10. USSR, Yakushev (Shadrin) 18:37.
Penalites: Kharlamov 14:45; Lapointe 19:41.

SHOTS ON GOAL

USSR: 10-10-10 – 30
Canada: 10-10-12 – 32

Goalies: USSR, Tretiak; Canada, Dryden.

Game 2: September 4, 1972

Maple Leaf Gardens, Toronto

The advent of game two prompted a flurry of activity on the Team Canada bench. Coach Harry Sinden beefed up his defense by adding a man to the blueline and switching to the older, more experienced Tony Esposito.

The team's three-week summer training camp had been at the Gardens and it was obvious they felt more comfortable there. Although there was no scoring in the first period of game two, Tony Esposito proved he was a good match for Kharlamov, stopping the Russian star on two impressive rushes.

At 7:14 in the second period, Phil Esposito started the scoring, followed in the third by Cournoyer and one goal each by the Mahovlich brothers. All the Soviets could muster was a single goal, just shy of six minutes into the third period.

Wayne Cashman, J.P. Parise and Bill Goldsworthy gave the Soviets a tutorial on the physical nature of the Canadian game, and the nation heaved a collective sigh of relief. 4–1 Team Canada.

Stats

Canada 4, USSR 1
Attendance: 16,485.

FIRST PERIOD
No scoring.
Penalties: Park 10:08; Henderson 15:19.

SECOND PERIOD
1. Canada, P. Esposito (Park, Cashman) 7:14.
Penalties: Gusev 2:07; Zimin 4:13; Bergman 15:16; Liapkin and Kharlamov (10-minute misconduct) 19:54.

THIRD PERIOD
2. Canada, Cournoyer (Park) 1:19.
3. USSR, Yakushev (Liapkin, Zimin) 5:53.
4. Canada, P. Mahovlich (P. Esposito) 6:47.
5. Canada, F. Mahovlich (Mikita, Cournoyer) 8:59.
Penalties: Clarke 5:15; Stapleton 6:14.

SHOTS ON GOAL
USSR: 7-5-9 – 21
Canada: 10-16-10 – 36
Goalies: USSR, Tretiak; Canada, T. Esposito.

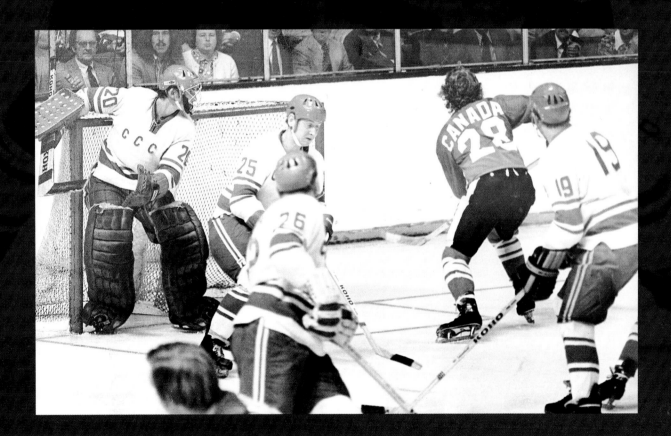

BOBBY CLARKE

Center Bobby Clarke, a baby-faced diabetic when he joined the Philadelphia Flyers in 1969–70, enjoyed a brilliant 15-year playing career that brought him to the Hockey Hall of Fame in 1987. He led the Flyers to Stanley Cup triumphs in 1974 and 1975, and captured the Hart Trophy three times. Other league honors include the Selke Trophy, the Bill Masterton Trophy and the Lester Patrick Trophy. His Hall of Fame induction was in 1987. Clarke is currently the president and general manager of the Flyers. He retired with 358 goals and 1,210 points in 1,144 games.

I was just 22 years old at the time. Just to go to camp with the top players in Canada was a thrill for me. I never really thought I was going to play that much. I was the last player they selected to come to camp, so just being invited was a huge honor. And then, of course, the series began and the competition, to our surprise, was so terrific. It seemed like the entire series was a rollercoaster – you're way down one moment and you have to figure a way to get back up. Then you win one and you're up on a high and you lose one, you're down again. It was a great experience for a young kid from Flin Flon.

I think that the elite level of competition separates some players. You find that some players who are great NHL players just aren't good enough at the level we found ourselves. On both teams, there were probably players like that. The quality and the level of play were so great from both sides.

I think there was a lot of arrogance on our part, with everyone feeling that we were going to beat the Russians eight straight games. As hard as the

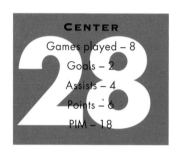

CENTER

28

Games played – 8
Goals – 2
Assists – 4
Points – 6
PIM – 18

coaches tried to prepare us, many of our players weren't in very good shape at the start. They hadn't worked too hard through camp and some of them felt like they were making a huge sacrifice just to be there, giving up part of their summer. Guys like Henderson and Ellis and me, if we were going to play any games, we had to work exceptionally hard, so our conditioning was probably better than a lot of the guys. We had some players who didn't work very hard and then when the series started, they just weren't ready for it. It took them all the way through Canada and into Sweden to get themselves into real good shape. That's why, for more than any other reason, we won in Russia.

There was an incident in game seven that was widely reported. I gave Valeri Kharlamov a tap on his sore ankle with my stick and he missed the final game. When journalist Dick Beddoes asked me about it, calling my shot "a wicked two-hander," I simply told him, "Dick, if I hadn't learned to lay on a two-hander once in a while, I'd never have left Flin Flon."

Clarke facing off with Aleksandr Maltsev.

The best thing that could have happened to Ronnie and me was to get this young kid making plays for us. He was terrific. We were the only line that played together in all eight games in that series. – *Paul Henderson*

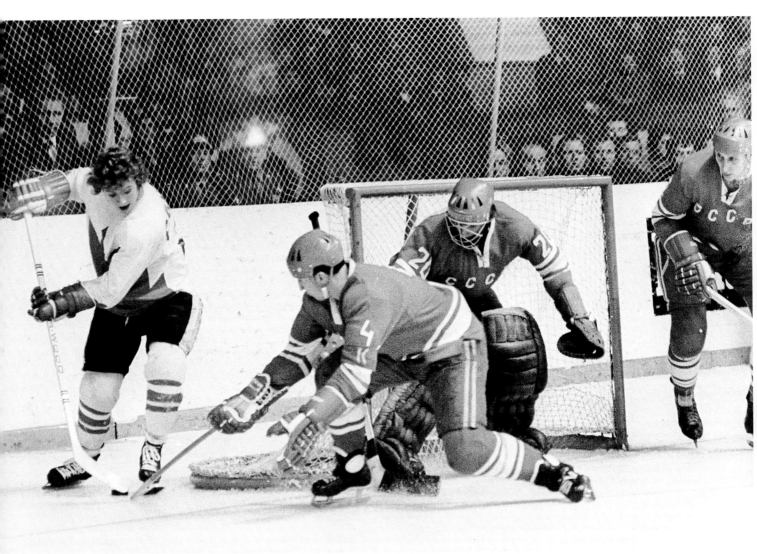

Clarke demonstrates his tenacious competitive spirit.

Team Canada '72 is right at the very top of my hockey life. I always considered winning the Stanley Cup more important, but certainly, they're close to being equal. Because of that series, I have some really good friends — very special friends I've had for 30 years because we competed together then. When you go through something like that, you get united with players. When you compete at that level and win with guys, you stay friends with them.

After that series there was all the talk about the Russian skill, the Russian passing and all this kind of stuff, but the reality of it is that the Russians had to change to the North American style before they could compete with us. They lost in '72; they lost in '76. The Russians, for all the great skills they supposedly had, didn't beat us very often.

There was an incident in game seven that was widely reported. I gave Valeri Kharlamov a tap on his sore ankle with my stick and he missed the final game. When journalist Dick Beddoes asked me about it, calling my shot "a wicked two-hander," I simply told him, "Dick, if I hadn't learned to lay on a two-hander once in a while, I'd never have left Flin Flon."

Dennis Hull clears the way for a Clarke attack.

When I quit playing, after spending my entire 15-year NHL career with the Flyers, I managed in Philly for 6 or 7 years. Then I went to Minnesota for 2 and Florida for another and I've been back in Philadelphia for 6 or 7 since. Basically, it's been 16 years of managing in the NHL.

Bobby Clarke finding time to autograph souvenir posters.

YVAN COURNOYER

Yvan Cournoyer, nicknamed "The Roadrunner" for his blinding speed, played on 10 Stanley Cup winning teams in Montreal. Back problems forced him to retire in 1978–79 but not before he'd amassed 428 goals and 863 points. He averaged just 17 penalty minutes per season. He was inducted into the Hockey Hall of Fame in 1982.

RIGHT WING
12
Games played – 8
Goals – 3
Assists – 2
Points – 5
PIM – 2

Well, the high point of the Summit Series for me was the last game – and the final goal – after coming back with the three games we had to win. When Paul Henderson jumped in my arms and said, "We did it! We did it!" – that was the very highest point of the series. We knew the expectations of the Canadian people. It was to win. We *had* to win. Sure, there was a lot of pressure. Everything to lose, nothing to gain – almost. It turned out to be a lot to gain because they [the Russians] turned out to be so good. At first, the pressure was very hard on us and I think that was the worst part of the entire series.

My only worry was to win. In Moscow, I didn't know what was going on back in Canada or what was happening anywhere else. I thought of nothing else but winning. I had no idea how monumental this series would turn out to be. When you win a Stanley Cup, you don't think about the parade the next day. You simply have to think of winning it. Whatever happens afterward is out of your jurisdiction.

I think Phil Esposito provided us with good leadership, but I think we were all very professional.

We came to be one team – a very solid team – and everybody did his best.

They had great players, too. They had Kharlamov, who was highly skilled. I had a chance to play against Yakushev, who was a big left winger and was also very good. Overall, they were a good team. Their goalie, Tretiak, was a surprise. The scouts said he was nothing. How wrong was that?

I think we should have been more prepared because the Russians had been doing very well in the Olympics and all the tournaments they were in. I have no idea why the scouting was so poor and badly organized. It was very hard on the players to fall behind and have to fight like hell to catch up. We wouldn't have had to wait until the last game to win it – if we'd been more prepared.

In the final moments of game eight, I was going to come off the ice because the coach had told us, "If the game is even and if you're tired and the puck is in their zone, you come to the bench and make a change." Well, I was very tired – I was at the end of a shift. That's when Pete Mahovlich was called to the bench by Henderson and Paul

Cournoyer flying in hot pursuit.

My only worry was to win. In Moscow, I didn't know what was going on back in Canada or what was happening anywhere else. I thought of nothing else but winning. I had no idea how monumental this series would turn out to be. When you win a Stanley Cup, you don't think about the parade the next day. You simply have to think of winning it. Whatever happens afterward is out of your jurisdiction.

The Roadrunner makes his way to the net.

jumped on the ice. I was going to come over too, but I changed my mind at the last minute. I decided to stay on the ice and take another shot at it. If the rink had been smaller – the size of our NHL rinks – I would have gone to the bench. But the rink was so wide and large, when I looked at the bench, it seemed so far away. I said to myself, "I might as well stay out here and see what happens." That's when I got the puck from one of the Russian defensemen. He tried to clear the zone, and I came back along the boards and intercepted the puck. I tried to throw it over to Paul and somebody tripped him, so he missed the puck and he flew into the boards in the corner. Then I saw Phil Esposito pick up the puck and fire it, and by then Paul had time to jump up and move in front of Tretiak. He shot once and shot again. The light flashed. I was right behind Paul when he scored the goal. If I'd had a camera, I could have taken the nicest shot of him. But he would have knocked

Cournoyer distracts Vladislav Tretiak, Moscow.

the camera from my hands because that's when he jumped into my arms and we began celebrating.

I often think if I hadn't changed my mind on that final shift, what would have happened? If I hadn't stayed on the ice, there wouldn't have been a Paul Henderson goal. Who would have been over by the boards to intercept the puck? Who would have kept it in the zone?

The Summit Series changed my life somewhat, like the Toronto series changed my life in '67 when we lost the Stanley Cup. In my years with the Canadiens [1963–64 through 1978–79], we were never afraid to lose and we were sure we were going to win. Obviously, in 1972, we didn't take the Russians seriously like we should have. This is what changed not just me but all of us, I

think. During that series, I learned how afraid you sometimes can be. A bit before the Summit Series, I told Frank Mahovlich, "Gee, Frank, I'm afraid. I don't know what to expect. We've never played these guys. I have no idea what they can do, and I don't like that. At least when you play in the play-offs, you know what to expect. We've never played the Russians before; we're not familiar with their style. I'm very afraid about the first game at the Montreal Forum."

In the six-team era, we would not talk to our opponent – on the ice or on the sidewalk outside the arena. It started to get better after that. In 1973, I won the Conn Smythe Trophy after I scored the winning goal for the Stanley Cup. Dennis Hull played a very good series for Chicago and if the

I asked Yvan Cournoyer after the game if winning in Moscow felt anything like winning the Stanley Cup. He said, "No, Dennis, this is 10 times better." So from then on, despite the fact I never managed to play on a Stanley Cup winner, I've always felt like I played on 10 of them.
– Dennis Hull

Cournoyer hunting for rebounds, Montreal.

Hawks had won the Cup, I think Dennis would have had a good chance to win the Smythe. In those days, we won a car with the trophy. The next year, I saw Dennis in an exhibition game — it was in the warm-up — and I said, "Dennis, your car is running very well!" He just laughed.

Winning the Stanley Cup and the Summit Series with Team Canada are very different. Winning in

Moscow was one of the thrills of a lifetime. With Team Canada, if you lose, you don't have a chance to come back. You represent your country for the first time. You have the flag on you. It's a completely different feeling from winning a Stanley Cup. For me, anyway. Two different events, completely different. But I place the two events tied at number one. I think that this is the ultimate

Cournoyer gets one by Tretiak.

achievement in hockey — winning the Stanley Cup and playing in the '72 series.

I've led a busy life after hockey. I had a restaurant in Lachine, Quebec, for about 12 years. I sold it 9 years ago. After that, I signed on with the Canadiens as the assistant coach to Mario Tremblay. Reggie Houle was the GM for a couple of years. Running the Roadrunners, my roller-hockey team, was a very good experience for me. It was a new sport to bring to Canada. When you can put 20,000 people in the Forum for the final game, I think that is very commendable. It was a great game to watch, too. The spectacle was incredible, because we went into two overtimes. The people who came out to see it really appreciated that. Even before that, I was working for the Montreal Canadiens as an ambassador for the team. This is what I'm doing now. I'm with them as an ambassador, along with Guy Lafleur, Henri Richard, Jean Beliveau and Reggie Houle. And it's always fun to go to the

Yvan Cournoyer at the Hockey Hall of Fame, 2000.

Molson Centre for a game. You feel like you're at home when you're with people who have been fans for so many years. They welcome you and say, "Nice to see you, Yvan." Sometimes they say, "We'll never forget Team Canada, Yvan." And I say, "Neither will I." And we both mean it. It feels very good. I mean very good.

MARCEL DIONNE

Marcel Dionne, with 731 career goals, remains third on the list of the NHL's top goal scorers, behind Wayne Gretzky and Gordie Howe. He topped 50 goals six times in his career (he played with Detroit, Los Angeles and New York) and was awarded the Art Ross Trophy in 1979–80. He starred on the Kings' Triple Crown Line with Charlie Simmer and Dave Taylor. He won the Lady Byng Trophy twice and represented Canada with distinction at four World Championships. Dionne retired after a brief stint with the New York Rangers late in his career, having amassed 1,771 points in 1,348 games. He was inducted into the Hockey Hall of Fame in 1992.

I was still just a rookie pro in '72, having just finished my first year in the NHL with the Detroit Red Wings. And even though I had a good season with the Wings (77 points in 78 games), I was still surprised to be named to Team Canada. There I was in training camp, rubbing elbows with all the stars of the NHL, veteran forwards like Phil Esposito and Frank Mahovlich, Yvan Cournoyer and all those other all-star players, men I would get to know a lot better in the years ahead.

CENTER
Games played – 0
34

I remember Phil and Frank and Yvan formed a line for the first game. And Harry Sinden kept the Rangers' GAG (goal a game) line of Rod Gilbert, Jean Ratelle and Vic Hadfield intact. Bobby Clarke clicked with Paul Henderson and Ron Ellis right from the start. There was another line of Mickey Redmond, Red Berenson and Pete Mahovlich. There were so many forwards on the team that I knew it was going to be very difficult for Harry Sinden and John Ferguson to decide who would play and who would sit. They had a problem fitting everybody in — guys like Dennis Hull, Wayne Cashman, Bill Goldsworthy, J.P. Parise, Stan Mikita, Gilbert Perreault and Richard Martin — and, of course, me. And it was the same with the defensemen.

In training camp, I think we were all a little uncertain about where we stood, with the coaches trying to form lines from all those players. And maybe there wasn't the intensity in training camp that there should have been because everybody was going around telling us the Russian players

Marcel Dionne relaxing at a reunion.

There's one other goal that stands out in my mind: Pete Mahovlich scoring shorthanded in game two, one of the prettiest goals I've ever seen.

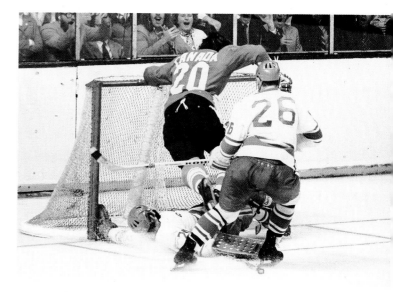

Peter Mahovlich scored in game two, the prettiest goal Marcel Dionne ever saw.

were amateurs and would be lucky to win one game from us.

Then the Russians gave us such a shock by winning the first game at the Montreal Forum. After they convinced us that they were first-rate players who could skate with us – they were in great condition and could match most of us in skills – I could understand it when Harry gave more ice time to the guys who'd been around for a while, the guys he was familiar with. So young players like me and Richard Martin and Gilbert Perreault and Dale Tallon had to wait our turn and hope we'd be needed. That was a little difficult for us because we all wanted to play. But we understood. At least I did. I just did what I was asked to do and enjoyed the company of these great stars. I figured I could learn a lot from them even by practicing with them.

Because I didn't play a prominent role in the series, some of my memories of those days have faded a bit. And while I'm very proud of what we accomplished as a team, I don't like to take credit personally. I have to credit the other guys for the success the team enjoyed, for the remarkable comeback in Moscow and for the unforgettable goal Paul Henderson scored in the final seconds of the final game. They all showed so much determination and guts.

There's one other goal that stands out in my mind: Pete Mahovlich scoring shorthanded in game two, one of the prettiest goals I've ever seen. And I remember the late Gary Bergman, my teammate in Detroit, playing defense as well as he ever played it in his life against the Russians. I could

say the same about Pat Stapleton and Bill White, both of whom seemed to anticipate so well what the Russian forwards were going to do next.

If I'd been around the NHL a little longer, with a couple more years under my belt, perhaps I would have been able to contribute a lot more in that series. Still, it was a unique experience to be part of it all and a real honor as a rookie NHLer to be on the team that created a hockey "first" – the best of our Canadian pros against the world's best amateurs, although they were hardly amateurs.

But they could play the game, couldn't they? And they might have won the series if the guys hadn't come together after the fourth game in Vancouver. Our team was in good shape by then, even though we lost that game, and everybody was pulling together. I think the guys all had a positive attitude by then and decided they had enough talent and pride and confidence to do the job in Moscow. And that's what they did, even though it took them until the last minute of the last game.

Today, I keep active with signings and a family sports-oriented business I manage in western New York near Buffalo.

KEN DRYDEN

Ken Dryden was originally the property of the Boston Bruins. After becoming a three-time All American at Cornell University, he joined the Montreal Canadiens in 1970–71. Called up for six games late in the season, he went on to lead the Canadiens to the Stanley Cup, defeating favored Boston and Chicago. Dryden captured the Conn Smythe Trophy that season and won the rookie award the following year – a hockey "first." His goaltending average of .758 is the best in NHL history. In retirement, he became Ontario's youth commissioner, and he authored *The Game*, hockey's all-time bestselling book. Inducted into the Hockey Hall of Fame in 1983, he now serves as president of the Toronto Maple Leafs.

Every team, if it is going to win, has to have a pleasant surprise. There's always somebody who comes through to excel, in part because those players that you count on, the other team knows all about and tends to focus on them. So it becomes really hard for a superstar to be a superstar in a Stanley Cup final. Often, somebody has to come almost from nowhere to excel and to surprise. Suddenly, in our case in '72, you have a Paul Henderson, who is that second or third line guy on a team who rises to deliver first line numbers offensively. And that generates such an immense energy kick for the team as a whole.

Phil Esposito might be called another surprise. Phil had been kind of a second banana wherever

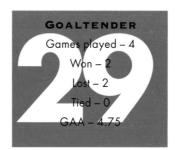

GOALTENDER
29
Games played – 4
Won – 2
Lost – 2
Tied – 0
GAA – 4.75

he played before, maybe third or fourth banana in Chicago. In Boston, as great as Phil had become, he (and everybody else) was going to be second banana to Bobby Orr.

Now when you put together a team like Team Canada, you don't know who your leaders are going to be. You can't even begin to predict it beforehand. Before that '72 series, people might have guessed that Phil Esposito would be a prominent player on the team, but to be the kind of leader that he turned out to be wouldn't have been anybody's guess. He hadn't needed to play that role before – the role wasn't there for him to play in either Chicago or Boston. And yet he absolutely was the leader in '72, the emotional and inspirational heart and soul of that team.

Phil is, and was then, a compelling figure. When he walks into a room, he's going to look to that room to direct itself toward him. But just because you have followers doesn't mean that you're a real leader. And while Phil was somebody

If I was nervous before game one in Montreal, by the time I reached game eight in Moscow, my legs and stomach were just jelly. I tried to settle myself down but it was almost impossible. But the game has a way of settling you down.

Vladimir Petrov puts the second puck past Dryden in the first game.

who was going to have followers on that team, it turned out he was a real leader, too.

We all remember game one in the Montreal Forum, where I had played so often for the Canadiens. I remember the incredible nervousness I felt before that first game but what I remember most clearly was after the first period. At that point it was a tie score: 2–2. But by then players on a team begin to get a feel for their opponents, and the feeling in that dressing room was one of, "Oooh, they are good. They are really, really good." This is in the first 20 minutes out of 480 minutes that make up eight games. And we knew even then that the remaining 460 minutes were going to be a great challenge for us, and very tough.

"Soviet amateurs shatter myth of Canadian pros' invincibility." That headline was printed promi-

nently by the Soviet news agency the following day. Our own reporters came up with words like "shocking," "disgraceful" and "disastrous."

And we, representing all Canadians, were embarrassed.

In training camp, we had watched a film of the Whitby Dunlops playing the Soviets back in the '50s. It seemed like a good idea at the time, but the film was too old, about 15 years old, and because Harry was in it, playing for Whitby, it allowed everybody in the room to make fun of Harry. So that was the kind of unintended impact that the screening had.

If I was nervous before game one in Montreal, by the time I reached game eight in Moscow, my legs and stomach were just jelly. I tried to settle myself down but it was almost impossible. But the game

Dryden takes in the big picture as his teammates apply pressure in the Soviet end.

has a way of settling you down. A lot of things that were almost out of control during the series, in the eighth and deciding game, got triggered rather easily. So all the debates and disputes over the referees and the kind of experience that all Canadian teams in international hockey have always had – Canada gets more penalties; we play a different kind of game; the rules are different – something that was simmering boiled over and exploded. J.P. Parise, always a nose-to-the-grind-stone kind of player, suddenly becomes the center of things, swinging his stick at the referee, stopping just before contact is made. Rod Gilbert in a fight – that's not Rod at all. Harry Sinden throws a chair on the ice. Pete Mahovlich rescues Eagleson.

Then, in the final seconds, Henderson's dramatic goal. He wasn't even supposed to have been on the ice in those critical seconds. Neither was Esposito perhaps, because he was at the end of a long shift. He would say later, "There was no way I was going off. It's gonna happen and I want to be part of it when it does."

I've been very fortunate to have played on six Stanley Cup winning teams in Montreal. But nothing in hockey ever brought me so low or took me so high. And nothing meant so much.

Looking back to that September in '72, we thought the series was going to be important because it was a first. That's where its importance was going to lie, that was its promise. But it didn't turn out that way. The importance turned out to be this incredibly close, passionate series, which was never the way it was supposed to have been.

We all have our memories, our experiences of those turbulent days. Some things remain important, others have faded from memory. I can hardly remember some of the Stanley Cups I won with Montreal. I remember some events from the first

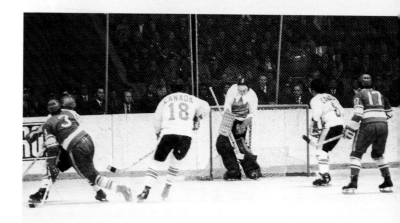

Top: Dryden stops Boris Mikhailov; middle: Jean Ratelle, Dryden and Rod Gilbert deny Vladimir Lutchenko and Valeri Kharlamov a scoring opportunity; bottom: Aleksandr Maltsev is shut down.

Dryden in Moscow.

one, and some events from my favorite Cup win when we beat Philadelphia four straight in '76. But neither the first one nor the '76 one is close to being as intense a memory as the Team Canada triumph in '72.

My guess is that most of the Russian players who played in the series, despite all the world championships and gold medals that they've won, may well feel about it with the same level of intensity as we do. I think most of them feel great passion for that series. You never have a winner and a loser feel so intensely about the same thing. But I think in this case it's true. We both won what we had to win. Team Canada had to win the series, whether it was 8−0 or 4−3−1. We had to win. What they had to win was a kind of respect, recognition that they could play and win, or potentially win, at the highest level of the game. And they absolutely won that.

I'm a sports fan and always have been, and I've followed the stories of Ralph Branca, who gave up that homer to Bobby Thompson in a mid-'50s

World Series when the Giants beat the Dodgers. And Bill Buckner, who was the goat of another World Series in Boston when a ground ball went right through his legs. When it comes to championships, the stakes are always so high. That's why I worried about being the most hated person in Canada if I turned out to be the goat in game eight in Moscow. And in hockey, the goalie is most likely to be the goat. You can be a Paul Henderson or a Phil Esposito, or you can be a Ralph Branca or a Bill Buckner. And your deeds, whether hero or goat, stay with you the rest of your life.

Ken Dryden and Phil Esposito.

RON ELLIS

Ron Ellis, known for his hard work and consistency, starred on right wing for the Toronto Maple Leafs for 15 seasons. He played in 1,034 games and scored 332 goals. He retired after the 1975 season but was persuaded to join Team Canada in 1976 and performed so well in the 1977 World Championship that he rejoined the Leafs for another 4 seasons.

RIGHT WING
Games played – 8
Goals – 0
Assists – 3
Points – 3
PIM – 8

The best memories of the Summit Series come to mind very quickly. The last three games, the three winning goals by Paul Henderson, the spectacular final goal – these are obvious highlights for sure. As for my own impressions of the series, the thing that comes to mind as a vivid memory is the first day of training camp, realizing, "Here I am, skating on the ice with the best Canadian-born players in the world." It was a real eye-opener. I was thrilled to be there, but it really didn't hit me until I was skating around with Esposito, Hull, Gilbert, Ratelle, Dryden, Lapointe and all the rest. That's a memory I'll always cherish.

I think Team Canada went into the series with a lot of confidence. I remember Bobby Clarke telling a reporter, "I look around and see the quality of the players here and wonder, who can beat us?" And few disagreed with him. Personally, I must say I was not quite as optimistic that we would win the series handily. The Russians were Olympic and world champions, and they had defeated some pretty good hockey clubs over the years. I had an opportunity to play against the Russians when I was in junior hockey. We had a great all-star team, and they whipped us so badly it was embarrassing. And that was a number of years prior to 1972. So there's no question that the Russians were developing fast as a hockey power. Even so, I felt in my heart we would succeed and we would win. But win all eight games? I wasn't at all certain about that.

I thought Don Awrey was a good competitor. He was a good, hard player and solid NHLer. I came down on him many, many nights and while we respected each other greatly, we didn't really enjoy playing against each other. I remember that first practice, I skated up beside him and I said, "Don, it's kind of nice to be on the same team for a change." Those memories are very special to me. To spend time with all those fellows and to almost go through war with them made it a special time in my life. I certainly respected all of them prior to that series, but getting to know them a little better, meeting their families, created a special bond between us all. The bond is very strong. I know that if a player from that team called me and needed my support or help, I'd be there. And I know he'd do the same for me.

On the Soviet side, I ended up spending most of my time on the ice covering a fellow by the name of Valeri Kharlamov. In my NHL career, I had to shadow a number of superstars – Bobby Hull being one of them. I would certainly put Kharlamov on the same level as Hull in terms of talent and ability.

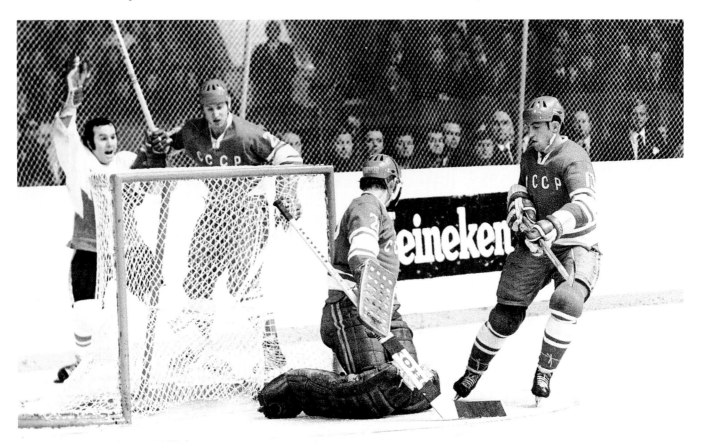

Ellis assists the first Canadian goal in game seven.

When we got home after the excitement of winning the series, training camps were already underway, so we dispersed very quickly and went to our teams. The next time we saw each other, we were playing against each other. So it was a fast transition we were forced to make. But from then on, there was something very unique about playing against these former teammates, and it lasted for my whole career. I call it respect. We played hard against each other but there was always that element of respect. You knew you weren't going to get a foul or a cheap shot from any one of those guys. From then on, when I came down on Awrey

we had some fun. He'd stop me or I'd get around him and there'd be a little wink, a little nod of the head. That would be the acknowledgment of what we'd shared together.

The low point of the series was the game in Vancouver. To be very blunt, we got booed off the ice by our own Canadian fans. Now that I've had time to reflect on it, I certainly don't hold anything against the fans in Vancouver. They were just as frustrated as we were. They thought they'd been assured that we would be winning all these games quite handily, and it wasn't happening. So they took their frustrations out on us. That was definitely a disappointment. Phil Esposito's speech at the end of the game, and everybody's reaction to it, was probably the turning point. Phil was the right guy to represent the team that night. Any one of us interviewed might have said something along the same lines, but not with the passion that Phil Esposito did. Everybody talked about that speech and said, "Wow! Maybe this Russian team is better than we thought. Maybe we've been caught off guard. Maybe it's time to get behind our guys." But that took a few days to happen. After the Vancouver game, we went back to Toronto, spent the night there, then headed off for Sweden. I found it hard to believe there was nobody at the airport to see us off. That was quite disappointing, because by then the guys were really putting out. We were all there for one reason, and that was to represent Canada.

Phil Esposito was our leader from day one. On the first day of camp, we rallied around Phil. It just seemed to happen very naturally. Then there was Paul Henderson – need I say more? Both Phil and Paul scored seven goals in the series, and they were all very important goals. The guys were picked co-MVPs and they deserved that honor, no question about it. But we had other players who came and answered the bell. One fellow who comes to mind is Gary Bergman, who played magnificently in all eight games. I think he was one of those fellows, like myself, who was invited to camp and thought he might get into a game or two. But his style of hockey was what we needed against the Russians – somebody who looked after the defensive end and didn't get caught in the Russian counterattacks. He had a wonderful series.

There were other guys that I thought played extremely well: Pete Mahovlich and Rod Gilbert and some of our defenseman – Bill White and Pat

Brad Park, Ellis and Paul Henderson at a practice at Toronto's Maple Leaf Gardens.

Stapleton did a wonderful job, as did Lapointe and Savard. The guys who played in most of the games had to be doing a good job to play in those games. But if I had to pick one guy who I was very happy for, that I think got a lot of respect from all the players, it'd have to be Gary Bergman – he'd be the guy.

On the Soviet side, I ended up spending most of my time on the ice covering a fellow by the name of Valeri Kharlamov. I was quite happy to take on that role as he was the Russians' key player. He was simply outstanding. We all agreed on that. In my NHL career, I had to shadow a number of superstars – Bobby Hull being one of them. I would certainly put Kharlamov on the same level as Hull in terms of talent and ability. Given the chance, he would have been a huge star in the NHL. Close behind him was a fellow named Yakushev. Everybody was impressed with him as well. He was a Frank Mahovlich-type player: a big reach, a good shot and always in the right spot at the right time. He got some goals against us that were devastating. He was strong and kept producing through the entire series. I was able to shut down

Bobby Clarke and Ellis surround Vladislav Tretiak as Vladimir Petrov looks on unable to help.

Kharlamov at times but Yakushev kept scoring game after game.

Their young goalie, Tretiak, is another opponent who impressed me with his coolness under pressure. Because of his play against us, he's now in the Hockey Hall of Fame. We made him look pretty good. He was a wonderful goalie, and he soon became a household name. They had some other fellows who made life difficult for us in that series: their captain, Mikhailov, and number 10, Maltsev. I was very impressed with both of them.

I have a memorable moment that was very unpleasant for me. In game six, the first of the three in a row we had to win, we were up 3–2 with about two minutes left in the game. And who takes a penalty? Ron Ellis. I'll never forget it. Let's say it was a questionable call – like a lot of them in the series. Still, I don't take penalties late in the game. I don't know if the refs were just trying to give the Russians one last chance or what. But there I was in the box, and it was surely the longest two

minutes of my life. I remember Paul Henderson telling me later that he looked over at me and thought how awful I looked – I looked ill and he felt sorry for me. It was a critical time. If the game ended in a tie, the series was over and they had won. But thankfully, Pete Mahovlich did a great job of killing off the penalty, and I was one happy hockey player when that happened. That is a memory that probably comes to me more often than Paul's dramatic goal in game eight.

When Paul scored, I was sitting on the bench ready to go out. As I recall it, with two minutes left to go in the game, our line came off. I remember Coach Sinden saying, "Get ready, you're going right back out there." So I was trying to get my breath and get pumped to go back out. Then he sent out the Phil Esposito, Yvan Cournoyer, Pete Mahovlich line while we were getting ready for one final go. He was going to give the Esposito line a chance to win it and then give us a chance. That's when Paul surprised us. He stood up and yelled at Peter for a line change. That's how Paul got on the ice ahead of Clarkie and me. And seconds later, Paul scored his famous goal. What a finish!

But there were still 34 seconds left in the game and a lot can happen in 34 seconds. We were deliriously happy but had to get control of our emotions. We had to settle down and finish the game. So after they called for the faceoff, Coach Sinden showed some confidence in me and sent me out with Pete Mahovlich and Phil Esposito to kill the last 34 seconds. The Russians tried hard but I can assure you, my guy wasn't going to get a chance to steal the game away from us. Perhaps the most memorable moment of all for me was just to be on the ice as those last few seconds ticked away.

Returning to the NHL after the series required an adjustment for a number of players. But not for me. I was able to enjoy my normal season that year. My game was fairly standard, and that's probably one of the reasons I was selected to play. I could play in both ends of the rink, and be called upon to stop a team from scoring late in the game. What's more, I was often able to pop a goal late in a game. I just came back to the Leafs and played my game and I think that season was quite consistent with other years I had. But it was a watershed experience for a number of guys. Bobby Clarke went on from that series to be a superstar. A young player like Marcel Dionne, just from being around the guys, took advantage of a real opportunity to grow and mature. He went on to be a superstar, and represented Canada so well for years and years after that.

After retiring from the NHL, I found it quite difficult to make the adjustment back to the real world. I went through a few years of trying to find my niche. I taught school for a little while, then I tried the insurance business. I even got into my own business for a few years. Finally an opportunity knocked on my door, one that allowed me to get back involved in the game. In 1991, I agreed to be part of a committee that ran the Canada Cup tournament. It was about that time that I met Scotty Morrison, who had been given the mandate to find a new home for the Hockey Hall of Fame. Scotty held a reception in a building that is now the Great Hall of the Hockey Hall of Fame, the room dedicated to the trophies and images of all Honoured Members enshrined in the Hockey Hall of Fame. The reception was to show the plans and announce the new location to the corporate world and others. Scotty invited the committee members from Team Canada to the event and I became quite excited about the whole enterprise. Some discussions with Scotty followed and I was asked to join the Hockey Hall of Fame staff as a

part-time consultant during the transition. When we moved into the new Hall, I was asked to stay on and I've been there ever since. My title is director of public relations and assistant to the president.

Ron Ellis at the Hockey Hall of Fame Team of the Twentieth Century induction in 2000.

I think the Summit Series had a big impact on my life. When it was all over and I had time to reflect, I think it did a lot for my confidence as a player. To say, "Gee, I was on the ice with the best in the world and I was able to hold my own and contribute" — that did a lot for my confidence when I came back to play in the NHL. It was an area that I had a little trouble with — wondering where I fit in. But as life has gone on, I just cherish the opportunity I had to be part of that team and represent Canada in something so special. We knew at the time that we were involved in a unique series, but I don't think any of us expected the legacy of it to live on as long as it has. In 2000, we were selected as the Team of the Century. The focus on that series never seems to end, and I'm so grateful that I was the right age and at the right time in my career to be selected to this team, because it's been a wonderful ride.

PHIL ESPOSITO

Phil Esposito, a Sault Ste. Marie native, rewrote the NHL record book during his brilliant career with Chicago, Boston and New York. He was the first player to surpass 100 points in a season. He guided Boston to Stanley Cups in 1970 and 1972. He once scored a league-record 76 goals in 78 games and captured the Hart Trophy twice, the Art Ross Trophy five times. He scored 717 goals during his 18-year career and was inducted into the Hockey Hall of Fame in 1984. Later he was manager (and coach briefly) of the New York Rangers and was the first manager of the Tampa Bay Lightning.

CENTER

Games played – 8
Goals – 7
Assists – 6
Points – 13
PIM – 15

In '72 when we played against the Russians, to say that we were unprepared for them is an understatement. We were not prepared for them at all. John McLellan – God rest his soul – was the one who went over and scouted the Russians. He came back and said they couldn't skate, couldn't shoot, couldn't pass and Tretiak, their goalie, couldn't stop a balloon. What he didn't know, I guess, is that they were all at Tretiak's wedding the night before he saw them play and they were in rough shape, especially Tretiak.

The series in Canada was very emotional for us. It was especially disappointing to hear the people boo us after the loss in Vancouver. And I tried to tell the country how we felt when I went on TV after that game. I told them I couldn't believe they were booing us. I told them the Russians had a good team and we were all trying our best. That we all agreed to play because we loved Canada. That's the reason we agreed to play.

We didn't really become a team until we got to Sweden. It happened in a cafeteria when Al Eagleson, John Ferguson and Harry Sinden came in and told us that they weren't going to let the wives come to Russia. At which point my brother Tony stood up and said jokingly, "Please let them come to Russia. Maybe the Russians will keep them." Finally I called a team meeting – players only – and we decided, "If the wives don't come over, we're not going to play." The guys running the show needed us more than we needed them. And

There will be no rest until the very last minute of the final game.

Vladimir Petrov tries to slow down Esposito.

Esposito and Yvan Cournoyer attack the Soviet goal crease, above, with positive results; below, after scoring the opening goal in Montreal, the pair celebrate.

we all agreed at that moment that we would simply come home if the wives weren't included. Nobody would go to Russia. Imagine the furor if that had happened. Eagleson panicked and said, "Listen, we've got to go to Russia." I was one of the captains on the team — me, Jean Ratelle and Frank Mahovlich. Poor Frank had a couple of nervous breakdowns on that trip. Anyway, we went in and talked to Harry and Fergie and Eagleson, and we said that unless everybody, including the wives, was included in the trip, we were going home. Simple as that. So everybody came along. I believe that was the first time we came together as a group. I mean every one of us agreed. Unanimous. And when the word got out, I think it was Harold

Phil Esposito did spectacular things out on the ice during that series. He would hold up big tough guys and just stand up to them instead of looking for that open spot like he usually did. He really played well defensively, and his offense was just excellent. He impressed me and became a great leader during that series. – *Stan Mikita*

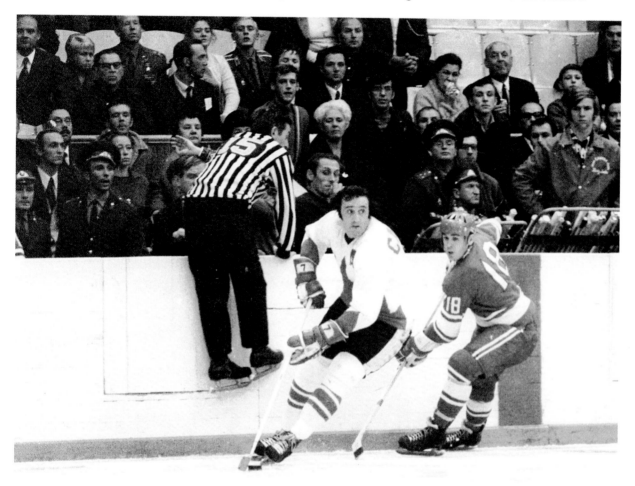

Esposito putting the moves on Vladimir Vikulov, Moscow.

Ballard who said, "Yeah, the wives will come over with mattresses strapped to their backs."

I'll always remember that first game in Russia. I was so damn nervous. The Russians gave us these stupid flowers in the pre-game ceremonies and I squeezed my flower so hard that I broke the stem. The whole world was watching when they introduced me. I stepped on the stem and fell flat on

my ass. I'll tell you, that broke some of the tension. But the ironic thing was, Brezhnev was president then and when I looked up, I made eye contact with him. There was the Soviet president staring right back at me. Everybody in the arena was laughing at my pratfall — everybody but him. His look was as cold as the ice I was sitting on. So I put my hand to my lips and, "smack," I blew him a kiss. And he still didn't laugh. But the guy

"To the people across Canada, we tried. We gave it our best. To the people who booed us, geez, all of us guys are really disheartened. We're disillusioned and disappointed. We cannot believe the bad press that we've got, the booing we've got in our own building. I'm completely disappointed. I cannot believe it. Every one of us guys – 35 guys – we came out because we love our country. Not for any other reason. We came because we love Canada."

Esposito was relentless throughout the series. Here he pressures Tretiak with another shot in Moscow.

beside him did and Brezhnev turned and gave him a look that almost paralyzed the poor guy. I said to myself, "Holy Christ, we may not get out of here alive."

We lost that game 5—4 after blowing a 4—1 lead. But nobody got down. I was proud of the way we played and I told the guys that was it, we weren't going to lose another damn game. We had finally come together and if we played them 10 more times we wouldn't lose a single game. And we didn't. They couldn't match our emotion. It was our kind of society against theirs and, man, that series turned into a war. I hated it over there.

Phil Esposito at the Hockey Hall of Fame.

We had airline pilots with us, and they told us that our hotel rooms might be bugged. We were told to be careful where we walked, and be careful what we said. Believe me, we went around cursing those Russians like you wouldn't believe. We figured that the microphones were everywhere. But the Air Canada pilots, of all people, were so paranoid that they were desperate to find these microphones. There was a rug in one of the rooms, and the pilots pulled it back. Underneath was a metal box with five screws holding it in place. Now you may have heard this story and how Cashman and I were said to have tinkered with this box, but I'm telling you it was the pilots.

One of them had a penknife, and he unscrewed those five screws. Then he discovered four more screws and when they came loose there was a tremendous crash in the ballroom below. What he

had done was unscrew the huge chandelier hanging from the ceiling. It's a wonder someone wasn't killed when it fell. It cost $3,800 to replace it. But we all pitched in and laughed about it later.

I sometimes wonder what it would have been like to have Gordie Howe with us in Moscow. He went over a couple of years later with the WHA team. What was he then, 46 or something? Gordie was something, boy. The toughest son of a bitch I ever played against. I played an old timers' game with Gordie one night and some guy was flying down the ice. Gordie leaned over to me and said, "You know, Phil, I think it's time we cut that guy down to size." Two minutes later, the guy was lying on the ice half-conscious and Gordie was leaning over him saying innocently, "Are you all right?" Christ, he just speared the guy right in the balls. It was unbelievable.

I remember one time watching the Dick Cavett Show when Gordie was on with his sons, Mark and Marty. Cavett says, "What kind of equipment did you wear, Gordie?" Gordie says, "Well, I wore skates, shin pads, elbow pads, pants and shoulder pads — and a cup, of course." Then Cavett says to the Howe boys, "Did you wear the same things?" They say, "Yeah, but we also wore helmets." And Cavett turns back to Gordie and says, "You never wore a helmet?" Gordie laughs and says, "Nah, I never wore a helmet." Cavett says, "But you wore a cup? Why would you wear a cup but not a helmet?" And Gordie says, "Hey, you can always get someone to do your thinking for you." Geez, I fell right out of bed when he said that.

CANADA

Game 3: September 6, 1972

Winnipeg Arena, Winnipeg

By now the Canadians had stopped taking the fleet-footed, superbly conditioned Soviet team lightly. To top it off, the Russian coaches were about to play an ace – three aces actually: they planned to use game three to set their so-called "kid-line" free. Yuri Lebedev, Aleksandr Bodunov and Viacheslav Anisin would combine for two goals and two assists as the Soviets fought Canada to a 4–4 tie.

Parise opened things up for the red-and-white just shy of two minutes into the first period, but the Soviets answered back less than two minutes later. Ratelle made it 2–1 Canada at 18:25.

Phil Esposito would stake Canada to a two-goal lead by scoring early in the second, but Kharlamov got one back eight minutes later. Henderson scored less than a minute after, but then the Russian "kid-line" found its stride and tied things up with two unanswered goals.

The third period was scoreless. By the end of game three, Canada had used two of the best goalkeepers the NHL had ever produced and had outshot their opponents 105 to 76. But a youngster named Tretiak had by then become a household name in Canada.

Things had become very serious.

Stats

Canada 4, USSR 4
Attendance: 10,600.

FIRST PERIOD
1. Canada, Parise (White, P. Esposito) 1:54.
2. USSR, Petrov (unassisted) 3:16.
3. Canada, Ratelle (Cournoyer, Bergman) 18:25.
Penalties: Vasiliev 3:02; Cashman 8:01; Parise 15:47.

SECOND PERIOD
4. Canada, P. Esposito (Cashman, Parise) 4:19.
5. USSR, Kharlamov (Tsigankov) 12:56.
6. Canada, Henderson (Ellis, Clarke) 13:47.
7. USSR, Lebedev (Vasiliev, Anisin) 14:59.
8. USSR, Bodunov (Anisin) 18:28.
Penalties: Petrov 4:46; Lebedev 11:00.

THIRD PERIOD
No scoring.
Penalties: White and Mishakov 1:33; Cashman (minor and misconduct) 10:44.

SHOTS ON GOAL
USSR: 9-8-8 – 25
Canada: 15-16-6 – 37
Goalies: USSR, Tretiak; Canada, T. Esposito.

Game 4: September 8, 1972

The Coliseum, Vancouver

Harry Sinden replaced Tony Esposito with Ken Dryden as his starter in goal and had to readjust his blueline, as veterans Serge Savard and Guy Lapointe were hurt. He tried to neutralize the lightening-fast Soviets with a total of five new players but to no avail.

The Soviets jumped out to a two-goal lead in the first period. Gilbert Perreault potted one for Canada a little more than five minutes into the second period, but the Russian juggernaut scored twice more before the end of the second. Things looked bleak indeed for the home side.

Bill Goldsworthy scored at 6:54 in the third. Aleksandr Yakushev then netted one for the Soviets. Finally, Dennis Hull added one more for Team Canada just before the end of the period. But it was too little too late for the Canadians. USSR 5, Canada 3.

Phil Esposito accounted for two assists in the game and would ultimately lead all scoring for the series but his biggest contribution was probably the TV interview he gave after the game. With Canadian boos still hot in his ears, he implored Canada to stick with his club: "If the Russians boo their players the way you have then I'll come back and apologize," he said. The statement struck a chord with Canadians from St. John's to Uclulet.

The Soviets had shocked the hockey world by winning two and tying one in the so-called hearth and home of hockey. Things started sounding cocky in the Russian dressing room. But the Canadians would regroup and the Russians were in for a battle "hot-stove" style.

Stats

USSR 5, Canada 3
Attendance: 15,570.

FIRST PERIOD
1. USSR, Mikhailov (Lutchenko, Petrov) 2:01.
2. USSR, Mikhailov (Lutchenko, Petrov) 7:29.
Penalties: Goldsworthy 1:24; Goldsworthy 5:58;
P. Esposito 19:29.

SECOND PERIOD
3. Canada, Perreault 5:37.
4. USSR, Blinov (Petrov, Mikhailov) 6:34.
5. USSR, Vikulov (Kharlamov, Maltsev) 13:52.
Penalties: Kuzkin 8:39.

THIRD PERIOD
6. Canada, Goldsworthy (P. Esposito, Bergman) 6:54.
7. USSR, Shadrin (Yakushev, Vasiliev) 11:05.
8. Canada, Hull (P. Esposito, Goldsworthy) 19:38.
Penalties: Petrov 2:01.

SHOTS ON GOAL
USSR: 11-14-6 – 31
Canada: 10-8-23 – 41
Goalies: USSR, Tretiak; Canada, Dryden.

TONY ESPOSITO

Tony Esposito, a former college goalie at Michigan Tech, following a brief stint with Montreal, won the Calder and Vezina Trophies in his first year as a Chicago Blackhawk. That season he recorded a modern-day record of 15 shutouts. When he retired after the 1983–84 season, Esposito, with 423 wins, trailed only Terry Sawchuk (447) and Jacques Plante (434). In retirement he worked with the NHLPA (National Hockey League Players' Association), the Pittsburgh Penguins as vice president and general manager and with the Tampa Bay Lightning.

I played in game two in Toronto and I feel I learned a lot by watching the Soviets in the opener a couple of nights earlier in Montreal when they shocked us with their speed and conditioning. I picked up on their style and decided I couldn't challenge them or I'd regret it. I hardly ever went out beyond my crease in the second game. I had to hang back and be really patient. If I went out after them, there was always the danger of getting trapped because they used their short passes so effectively.

The Russians were two different teams, one team when they went ahead in a game and a much different team when they fell behind. After the big goal in game two scored by Peter Mahovlich — a shorthanded effort, a beautiful goal — from then on they had to play catch-up hockey. I knew what was at stake and I knew I had to come up with a

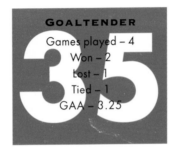

GOALTENDER
35
Games played – 4
Won – 2
Lost – 1
Tied – 1
GAA – 3.25

big effort. We dictated the pace of that game and we were able to skate off with a win. I'm sure the whole country felt better when we skated off the ice that night.

I played again in game three in Winnipeg and it was a pretty even hockey game – a 5–5 tie. But I let in one bad goal and that really ticked me off. You couldn't afford to give up a bad goal against those guys. The puck went right through my legs. If I'd stopped that one we might have won the game.

We got stronger as the series moved along even though we played poorly in Vancouver. When we went overseas, we became more competitive and less chippy. We focused on hockey and our top guys didn't let themselves become too emotional. They stayed cool — you know, let's take care of business and win the game. Less yapping at the referees. Even though we lost game five in Moscow after taking a 3–0 lead, we could see some things happening that gave us some confidence. The Russians couldn't seem to maintain their intensity and I noticed some cracks in Tretiak's play. Then

I picked up on the Soviet style and decided I couldn't challenge them or I'd regret it. I hardly ever went out beyond my crease in the second game. I had to hang back and be really patient.

In game three in Winnipeg it was a pretty even hockey game – a 5–5 tie. But I let in one bad goal and that really ticked me off. You couldn't afford to give up a bad goal against those guys. The puck went right through my legs. If I'd stopped that one we might have won the game.

again, he might have been saying the same about me. I'm not used to losing when I have a 4–1 cushion with 11 minutes to play. They squeezed out a 5–4 win. They named me one of the stars of that game but I didn't think I deserved the honor, not after giving up five goals in the third period.

Still, the pressure was mounting on Tretiak and by the sixth and seventh games he was starting to fight the puck. In the final game he let in a couple of bad goals. That was good for us. But there's no question he cracked. I felt I played well in game

seven, a crucial game for us. It made up for the bad third period I suffered through in game five. We had to win it and we did.

I thought I might get the starting assignment in game eight. I don't second-guess coaches but if it were me making the coaching decisions I would have said, "Let's go with Tony in game eight. He's coming off his best game in game seven." But Harry Sinden and John Ferguson decided to go with Dryden and that was all right by me. It's a

Gary Bergman blocks potential trouble as Tony "O" keeps his eyes on the puck, Moscow.

team game and they did what they thought was best. And we won it, which is the important thing.

The Russian player who impressed me most was Yakushev. He was a great playmaker and shooter. He'd try to get you to come at him and then he'd make a slick little move and make you look foolish. I was always aware of him when he was on the ice.

On Team Canada, thank goodness somebody took the bull by the horns on our team and became our leader. Fortunately, my brother Phil did that and no team has ever had better leader-

ship. It had to be a player with stature who came forward. If a third or fourth line guy had tried to become our leader, I'm sure someone would have said, "Hey, who are you? Sit down."

We could have used Bobby Hull in that series. He would have given us some great offense. But the feeling seemed to be that we could win without him. The organizers badly underestimated the Russians. It was all politics, of course. Bobby jumped to the WHA that summer. But he would have looked good in one of our uniforms.

When we went overseas, we became more competitive and less chippy. We focused on hockey and our top guys didn't let themselves become too emotional. They stayed cool . . . let's take care of business and win the game. Less yapping at the referees.

As for the guys who quit and left for home, I'll wager they're kicking their asses over that. They could have been part of it and they weren't around at the finish. And that series has become bigger and bigger as the years go by.

T. Esposito
70

The Russian player who impressed me most was Yakushev. He was a great playmaker and shooter. He'd try to get you to come at him and then he'd make a slick little move and make you look foolish.

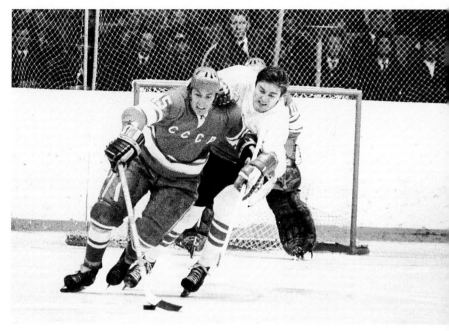

Aleksandr Yakushev, with Peter Mahovlich after him.

Pat Stapleton, Peter Mahovlich and Bill White scramble after the puck as it slides toward Esposito, Moscow.

T. Esposito

71

Tony and Phil Esposito in an on-ice interview with Johnny Esau.

I finished my NHL career in 1983–84. Sixteen
years is a good long time at that level, 15 of them
with the Chicago Blackhawks. Then I did some
work with the NHLPA, until I was offered a job
with Pittsburgh as general manager in 1988. I was
with the Penguins for a couple of years and then
Phil, who helped establish NHL hockey in Florida,
brought me to Tampa Bay in the early '90s. He
was the first general manager of the Lightning
and a couple of years later some wealthy people
came around and bought us out. Now I do some
work with Ficel Marketing and some speaking
engagements. I enjoy getting around and meeting
the fans. I notice that anyone middle-aged or older
always mentions that big series in 1972. There'll
never be another one like it and I was proud to be
a part of it.

Phil and Tony Esposito in 1997.

JOHN FERGUSON

John Ferguson was invited to join Team Canada as a player in 1972 but declined, serving as assistant coach of the team instead. He joined the Montreal Canadiens in 1962 (his contract purchased from Cleveland) and in the following eight seasons he played on five Stanley Cup winners. From 1976 to 1978, Ferguson was manager of the New York Rangers. He joined the Winnipeg Jets of the WHA in a similar position in 1978–79. His team won the Avco Cup that year and he stayed with the Jets until 1989. He was part of the Ottawa Senators' front office from 1992 to 1995 and has been scouting for the San Jose Sharks since 1995.

ASSISTANT COACH

The decision not to play for the team was a tough one to make. Harry had chosen me to play right away and that would have been a real experience for me. Then we had those well-publicized difficulties with Bobby Hull who was barred from the team because he had jumped to the World Hockey Association. Because I had retired, I would have had to sign an NHL contract to be a player on the team. So Harry asked me to become assistant general manager and assistant coach.

I was not disappointed that [Bobby] Hull didn't come along because I knew the players we had like Dennis Hull, Frank Mahovlich and Vic Hadfield were solid left wingers. We also had Wayne Cashman and Jean-Paul Parise, so we were quite sure we could do the job without him.

We had lost the first game and we thought at that time we had played our 20 most superior athletes. We didn't go into the game with a team concept at all. We had our highest scoring lines trying to do the job but we needed a team strategy.

Before or after game two in Toronto, Hadfield, Gilbert and Ratelle went in to see Harry. Vic was particularly upset because he wasn't playing. That was the start of the problems with Vic and Harry and eventually Vic would quit the team. We had lost the first game and we thought at that time we had played our 20 most superior athletes. We didn't go into the game with a team concept at all. We had our highest scoring lines trying to do the job, but we needed a team strategy.

The highlight of the experience for me was being there and winning — without a doubt. And my relationship with Harry Sinden kept growing all the time. We were the two best guys for the job and I really came to love Harry's knowledge of hockey. He had wisdom beyond his years. When we selected the team, neither one of us showed favoritism. I persuaded Harry to take Serge Savard even though he had just come off a broken leg, but he was still one of the premier defenseman in the National League. He played in every game we won. A couple of young guys surprised us during training camp. We put Ronnie Ellis, Bobby Clarke and Paul Henderson together, and they just fit like a glove.

There was one player on the Soviet side who really ticked me off – Boris Mikhailov. He really upset me. He kicked Gary Bergman and Yvan Cournoyer and tried to intimidate some other guys. He came by the bench and I let him have it. I didn't throw a punch at him but I called him a dirty name and ended up getting a bench penalty.

Gary Bergman and Boris Mikhailov.

My lowest moment was going to Vancouver, my old hometown, and having the fans boo us. That was tough to handle but Phil made a great speech on TV and told the public how we all felt. But we finally became a team when we went to Sweden for seven or eight days, and the boys bonded really well. There was talk of bringing the wives over at that time but we had work to do. We were behind the eight ball and we didn't want any distractions. We decided instead for them to join us when we got to Russia.

There was one player on the Soviet side who really ticked me off – Boris Mikhailov. He really upset me. He kicked Gary Bergman and Yvan Cournoyer and tried to intimidate some other guys. I said at the time that he wouldn't last a game in the NHL – he would be challenged and fought every time he stepped on the ice. They (the NHL players) would get him and finish his hockey career. He came by the bench and I let him have it. I didn't throw a punch at him but I called him a dirty name and ended up getting a bench penalty.

When I came back from that series, Boston wanted me to come and play for them right away. Then I was offered a job as the playing coach for the Los Angeles Kings. Eventually I decided to go to New York as a general manager and then coach. That's when I went after Anders Hedberg and Ulf Nils-

son, two Swedish stars in the WHA. I brought them to New York with a lot of fanfare. When I left, I spent the next 12 years in Winnipeg. Then I ran the Windsor Raceway for 3 years. After that I went back into hockey management with the Ottawa Senators as director of player personnel. I wasn't happy in Ottawa because we couldn't get players signed. I left, and got a call from Dean Lombardi who asked me if I wanted to take over the professional scouting for the San Jose Sharks. They were ranked dead last at the time and now we are a very respected team. I really enjoy my role there.

When I came back from Moscow I had a prized possession with me – a souvenir hockey stick that was signed by a lot of the Russians and all of Team Canada. It was a personal thing that I wanted to

John Ferguson was an excellent choice to help coach Harry Sinden behind the bench. There's a famous story about how we were all on a float in Montreal and we called Prime Minister Pierre Trudeau aboard. I took Fergie's stick, signed by all the players, and gave it to the Prime Minister. I told him Fergie wanted him to have it. Fergie was fuming. I believe Fergie got the stick back, but I'm not sure of that. – *Serge Savard*

Ken Dryden, Ferguson and Yvan Cournoyer.

bring home. I had it in my hand and when Prime Minister Pierre Elliott Trudeau met us when we left the plane, Serge Savard pulled the stick out of my hand and said, "Look what John Ferguson brought you, Mr. Prime Minister." And much to my amazement, Trudeau accepted it. Years later, Pierre sent me this letter:

Dear Mr. Ferguson,
I regret that due to a friendly prank of your teammate Serge Savard I ended up with your autographed hockey stick. It was fun having it for a while, but I really did not intend to keep it. In returning it to you, may I reiterate my congratulations on your fine performance as assistant coach for victorious Team Canada.

Best regards,
Sincerely
Pierre Elliott Trudeau

I sent the stick back to Trudeau, suggesting that it might be useful during his election campaign at that time. He wrote me back this letter:

Dear Mr. Ferguson,
Thank you for your letter of good wishes, and for sending me the autographed stick. You suggested that I might need it for the election campaign and perhaps I should have made better use of it at that time. However, it may be more valuable to me in the

coming weeks if we are not to be shut out of the series. My own team will meet to rally its forces, overcome a few painful defeats and learn to outplay the opposition. What better encouragement than a stick signed by the members of Team Canada.

With my best regards,
Sincerely
Pierre Elliott Trudeau

So Pierre ended up keeping the stick after all.

Let me say a word about Paul Henderson, who came through in the clutch for us throughout the series and especially in that final game in Moscow. Paul was the ideal guy to score the winning goal. Some people have mocked him for his born-again Christianity but I think he is a model citizen, a very presentable guy who talks to everybody, has time for everybody, and he never had a big ego that put him higher than anyone else. Becoming a hero like he did, getting all that acclaim, could have been a tough thing to handle for some people. But Paul has handled it really well.

John Ferguson signs memorabilia at the Royal York Hotel, Toronto.

ROD GILBERT

Rod Gilbert survived a broken back suffered in junior hockey to spend his entire 15-year NHL career with the New York Rangers, where he set 20 team scoring records. When he retired in 1977, his stats of 406 career goals and 1,021 points were second only to Gordie Howe among the league's right wingers. He was a key figure on the Rangers' famous GAG (goal a game) line along with Vic Hadfield and Jean Ratelle. Gilbert is still known as "Mr. Hockey" among New York Ranger fans. He was elected to the Hockey Hall of Fame in 1982 and now serves the Rangers as director of community relations.

I remember being very emotional that summer of 1972 because the year before I had gotten into arbitration with Emile Francis, my boss with the Rangers. The arbitrator had given me less than Francis had offered, and I had my best season in 1971–72 with 43 goals. Then I made the first all-star team and I became free after that because I just had a one-year contract. I was a little bit upset that even after my best season Francis didn't come up to me and say, "Look, Rod, you had a really good season. You were right about what you asked for and the arbitrator screwed you." But he didn't do that and he left me out in the open. During that time, Nick Milleti from Cleveland with the WHA came to me with an offer which was four times more than what Francis had offered.

We were going to Toronto where the Team Canada members were to be introduced and I was traveling with Jean Ratelle when he suddenly tells me he just signed with the Rangers. He agreed to $90,000 a year for four years. Now I know Francis is not going to give me more than $90,000. Maybe a little bit more, but not like Cleveland's $300,000.

RIGHT WING
Games played – 6
Goals – 1
Assists – 3
Points – 4
PIM – 9

And then I was chosen to represent Canada with all these star athletes and that was exciting. But I couldn't really face the fact that I was going to play for $90,000 in the NHL when I could play for $300,000 over in Cleveland for five years. And it was all guaranteed money! So I was confused and excited and upset all at the same time.

I came back to New York and I decided to see Francis and I told him what Cleveland was offering me. He almost choked. I said, "I want $300,000 otherwise I'm no longer a Ranger." So he ran upstairs and spoke to [Ranger president] Bill Jennings and he got me the money. But then he had to upgrade Jean to $300,000, and Vic Hadfield too, who had signed for $50,000. Goalie Ed Giacomin got a big upgrade and Brad Park's salary

I was so disappointed because we didn't control the puck once during my shift and then we had to change! I didn't even touch it. The whole line didn't get the puck. I said, "I think we're in trouble here. I hope the next shift gets better." But it didn't. We lost 7–3.

I played all four games in Russia. The biggest moment was when we won game eight, of course. I made a play to Bill White to tie the score at three all. Then I had a fight – the only fight of the series. I nailed this big Russian but he didn't even go down. I've got a picture of Dennis Hull and Bill White laughing their heads off at me because I was underneath this guy and I was yelling, "Please get this big gorilla off me!"

Gilbert waiting for a rebound opportunity despite being leaned on by another "gorilla."

was boosted to $300,000. So I brought all these guys up with me. That was how I got to play for Team Canada — because you had to have an NHL contract before you could play. Bobby Hull, Gordie Howe, Derek Sanderson and J.C. Tremblay had all jumped to the WHA so they became ineligible.

My worst moment was when we played the first game and Ratelle and Hadfield and I were on the ice for the first time, and Esposito and Cournoyer had scored the first two goals. I really wanted a

chance to score. I had my parents in the stands, my sister, my brother and some friends. And I was so disappointed because we didn't control the puck once during my shift and then we had to change! I didn't even touch it. The whole line didn't get the puck. I said, "I think we're in trouble here. I hope the next shift gets better." But it didn't. We lost 7–3. And after the game, my lowest moment was when my brother came up to me — he's six years older and my mentor, and he really motivated me when I was a kid — and said, "You are a disgrace to your country, a disgrace to YOUR COUNTRY!" I was in shock. My own brother! He said, "You're all a bunch a bums." I told him we tried as hard as we could but the other team was just a little bit better than us.

I played all four games in Russia. The biggest moment was when we won game eight, of course. I made a play to Bill White to tie the score at three all. Then I had a fight — the only fight of the series. I nailed this big Russian but he didn't even go down. His name was Evgeni Mishakov, number 12. He kicked me in the back of the leg. We were losing with only nine minutes to go, and I came on the faceoff, dropped my glove and just hammered him. He didn't even move. He weighed 240 pounds and he was 5'8", and he grabbed me and body-slammed me into the ice. I've got a picture of Dennis Hull and Bill White laughing their heads off at me because I was underneath this guy and I was yelling, "Please get this big gorilla off me!" I didn't try to hit him again because I would have been thrown out of the game. No one saw anything, anyhow.

And then we got the win and that was exhilarating, emotional and very satisfying because they were doing all this shit to us over there. They stole our food and our beer. Can you beat that, stealing our beer?

When Vic Hadfield left the team I was really upset. Vic had already shown his displeasure about not playing — and rightfully so — after the second game. We had 35 guys and we lost badly in Montreal, then we came back to Toronto. We didn't play in Toronto because our line played in Montreal. But Vic's from Toronto. He had scored 50 goals the year before and our line was number one in the NHL. So he expected to play. We practiced that morning but noticed that our names were not on the board for

that night. So the three of us went in to see Sinden and Vic spoke out. He said, "Look, are you blaming us for the loss in Montreal? Is that why we're not playing?" Harry didn't know what to say. Finally he said, "Well, we're not blaming you directly, but there's 35 guys here and we've got to make some changes because it didn't work in Montreal. So I'm going to put a different type of player out there." That really made Vic upset and he stayed behind and had some words with Sinden.

An odd thing happened after we lost the fourth game in Vancouver 5–0 and got booed by the fans there. I was walking down the street with Frank Mahovlich and Ratty [Ratelle], and Mahovlich was saying to us, "Take a look across the street at those two guys. They're following us." I insisted they weren't but he kept saying, "Those two guys are KGB and they're following us." I said, "Frank, those two guys were just at the game, they're fans, they're not following us." And then Frank just lost it. He had a bit of a nervous breakdown and they put him in the hospital. So then we went to Sweden, and Vic and me and Ratty were all playing really well. We figured we were going to be reunited for the game against the Russians. And it was that day Harry told Vic that he decided to reinsert Frank into the lineup and put Dennis Hull with me and Ratty. Vic was dropped from our line. So he packed up and left after that. We didn't react. We had to play the four games in Russia. We just shut up and played. What else could we

And then we got the win and that was exhilarating, emotional and very satisfying because they were doing all this shit to us over there. They stole our food and our beer. Can you beat that, stealing our beer?

Jean Ratelle and Gilbert beat Aleksandr Maltsev to the puck in Moscow.

do? And it's a good thing we did, because we made the difference, Ratty and I.

I remember going for my second back surgery. The doctor that supervised the first operation was the Rangers' orthopedic surgeon. But the chairman of the board of the Rangers was a firm believer in the Mayo Clinic. So when he found out that the best prospect in the organization had gotten injured, instead of sending me back to the doctor to perform the operation he chose to send me to the Mayo Clinic.

But the Mayo Clinic screwed up. They took a bone from my tibia in my leg, instead of from my pelvis, and instead of taking an hour for the operation, they took five and a half hours. When my blood didn't coagulate, they put me in a hospital room with three other patients who were worse off than me. One had a leg amputated. Then I developed an infection and the graph readings didn't take solidly. So everything was a disaster. When I went to see the team surgeon, he took X-rays and said casually, "Next time I'll fix it."

I was just pissed. I thought there's not gonna be a next time because I'm not going through that again. So I played for another four years. Then, just like he predicted, the graph broke in my back and I was paralyzed all over again. This time he took me into the hospital, operated on me for an hour and a half, took a bone from my pelvis, fused three vertebrae with the interweaving method and made a solid piece in my back so that I could never bend from there again.

Also, in order to prevent the infection that was continuously bothering me at the time, he was feeding me seven antibiotic pills every four hours. I didn't get any food, just water through intravenous. And suddenly for a week I couldn't digest the pills anymore. One day Emile Francis and Bill Jennings came to visit me. The pills lodged in my esophagus and I started to choke to death while they were watching. I just couldn't breathe anymore. I suddenly went blue and then fainted and somebody called the nurse.

Then I was unconscious, and when I opened my eyes I realized that I was out of my body in the corner of the room. The nurse came up and said, "We lost him, I can't find his pulse, somebody help me, please help me!" I stood watching as the doctors came in with the electrodes to jolt my heart back to life. Finally they put something in my mouth to get the pills dislodged and I was able to cough everything out. Suddenly I started to breathe again. It must have taken about four or five minutes. In the meantime, I heard every conversation as I was standing out of my body. Francis was yelling at the nurse, "Bring him back, damn it, he's my best player." And I was still out, no pulse, no breathing, nothing. It was a weird feeling as I watched everyone work on me, trying to revive me.

After the out-of-body experience, I didn't tell anyone about it. It was so different, and I didn't think anyone would believe me. I just kept it to myself.

The impact that series had on me was that it reassured me of my capabilities. It was the highest level of accomplishment and joy for me. For the previous 10 years, I had been working really hard, and after my back injury and surgery, I wanted to establish myself as a top player in the NHL. I wanted to play well and be a leader on the Rangers. But we could never get a sniff of anything. I couldn't imagine what was coming next. I never gave up, though. And then in the early '70s we made it to the semifinals and beat some great teams in the playoffs. But we just never won the Cup.

So the Team Canada series showed me what it feels like to actually win something really big for a change. And I considered myself very fortunate because there was a time I figured my career was all over.

Rod Gilbert in 1997.

BRIAN GLENNIE

Brian Glennie joined the Toronto Maple Leafs in 1969–70 after three solid seasons with the junior Marlboros and minor league stints in Rochester and Tulsa. He was a regular on the Leaf blueline for the next nine years and then was traded to the L.A. Kings for a final season in 1978–79. He played in 572 NHL games and compiled 114 points.

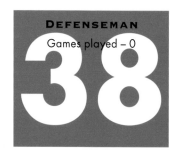

DEFENSEMAN
Games played – 0
38

The most lasting memory I have is the reaction of the Canadian fans after Paul Henderson scored the goal that shook the hockey world. The Canadian fans up in the stands in Moscow, 3,000 strong, waving the flags and singing "O Canada" – my, oh my, I'll never forget that. Never! It was such an emotional series and to go down to the end like that certainly is ingrained in my mind forever.

And the reception we received when we got back to Canada – I had no idea what was happening back home as a result of that victory. We were so isolated over there. We didn't realize our triumph had become such a huge story in Canada.

The downside of the series for me was all the off-ice stuff. It was watching soldiers stepping on kids' hands when we were throwing gum to them off the bus. I remember the guys getting off the bus and walking out and giving the kids a pack of gum in front of the soldiers and telling them to take off with it. And seeing the soldiers in the stands not knowing how to control the Canadian fans, trying to get the cowbell and them passing it around. It's just a different way of life over there. It was the first time they had ever allowed that many people from a foreign country into Russia all at once. All the politics that got involved, all the political stuff that they tried to do off the ice to upset us, it became almost bigger than the games, which was unfortunate.

To give you an example of the isolation, and this is a true story, I think it was about Christmas-time after we got back and it was all over, my wife Barbara had a good friend who had relatives in the Ukraine about 500 miles outside of Moscow. Her

The Canadian fans up in the stands in Moscow, 3,000 strong, waving the flags and singing "O Canada" – my, oh my, I'll never forget that. Never!

friend received a letter from her relatives over there and she brought it over to our house and read it to us. Basically what the letter said was how sad it was, that in the great hockey confrontation between Canada and Russia, Canada had lost eight games to zero! That showed how much they controlled the media.

When we were at a dinner at the Canadian embassy one night, there was a picture of somebody lying on a park bench. I asked one of the embassy staff who could read Russian to explain it to me. And basically, it was a picture saying, "Why would you want to live in Canada where you aren't guaranteed a home? In Canada, you have to sleep on a park bench." It was a tremendous culture shock, seeing the various ways they tried to downgrade our way of life and upgrade theirs. There was incredible control over there — just a total lack of freedom. They are the things that I remember now of the overall experience.

On the brighter side, there were many, many moments I cherish — Peter Mahovlich's goal in Maple Leaf Gardens; Phil's speech in Vancouver; the goosebumps I felt when the Canadian fans sang "O Canada."

We left Canada on a very down note. We were being booed by our own fans and it seemed like the lowest point possible. I don't think we underestimated them. We might have, but I certainly didn't because I had played against them before in the Olympics in 1968 in Grenoble, France. Also, I played on the Toronto Marlie team, I think it was around 1966, when we added two players, Derek Sanderson and Bobby Orr, and they played well against us. So I had lots of experience against the Russians. I wasn't surprised by their goaltending, either, because in 1968, we lost the final game to the Russians. All we had to do was tie the game to bring home the gold medal and we ended up

Glennie, Ron Ellis and Paul Henderson with their wives, taking in the sights of Moscow.

getting the bronze. We couldn't put a pea past their goaltender — I'm not sure if it was Tretiak, but their goaltending was unbelievable and they ended up beating us 5—0.

When we first got to training camp, we were enemies. There were some frosty looks exchanged but they soon disappeared and we all got along famously. I thank Dallas Smith every day for turning down the opportunity to play. That's how my name was added to the list, down near the bottom. It became one of the greatest events of my life.

I must admit, I wasn't a big fan of Phil Esposito's at the beginning of training camp. Toronto and Boston had had some playoff wars and it was my job to get him out from in front of the net. But I

On defense, little Patty Stapleton and big Billy White were huge for us, not only for their on-ice skills but for their sense of humor off-ice. I mean, they had Canadian fans and players looking for a mythical Chinese restaurant the whole time.

never realized how good a player Phil really was. There were times when he picked us up and carried us and I have tremendous respect for him now. Then, of course, there's the supposed checking line of Clarke, Henderson and Ellis. What can you say about those three guys? They just played their hearts out the whole time, as everybody did on the team. On defense, little Patty Stapleton and big Billy White were huge for us, not only for their on-ice skills but for their sense of humor off-ice. I mean, they had Canadian fans and players looking for a mythical Chinese restaurant the whole time because all the fans were unhappy with the food.

Once we got into the thick of it, I came away with a lot of respect for the players who didn't dress. In the heat of those torrid battles, Harry had to go with the guys who were playing game in and game out. It would be very difficult, in the seventh or eighth game, to inject somebody new into the line-up, somebody who hadn't played since the second game or hadn't played at all. On the other side, I admired Kharlamov who, unfortunately, couldn't play the eighth game. He was knocked out of commission by Bobby Clarke's hit across the ankle.

I'm sitting here looking at my Team of the Century trophy and I've got my Olympic bronze medal around it. I believe the series made me a much better hockey player. Even though I didn't play against the Russians – I played against the Swedes and Czechs – I practiced with the best players in the National Hockey League for that entire period of time. I practiced with Bobby Orr every day, and

believe me, if Bobby's knees had been good, I don't think it would have taken that long for the results to be in Canada's favor. In junior I watched him dominate the game we lost to the Russians 2–1, but he was the best player on the ice by far. Working with these greats of the game made me a better hockey player. It gave me more confidence. Unfortunately, my career ended with a back injury after nine years with the Leafs and a final season with the Kings. But no one can ever take the fabulous memories away from me. It was just a wonderful experience to have been part of that team, although my name may often be used in a hockey trivia quiz.

Brian Glennie at a golf tournament in 1999.

I got into the restaurant business after I retired. I had a restaurant called Wheels on Church Street in Toronto. Then, I had a hotel/bar in Muskoka called Inn on the Bay. Unfortunately for me, it turned out to be a very tough business and I suffered through a bankruptcy. Then I started all over again and I got into the printing business with a wonderful company called York Litho. It became a division of Maclean-Hunter and is now part of Transcontinental Printing. Unfortunately, I have encountered some health problems over the years and they have shot me down. So I'm basically retired and living in Muskoka for medical reasons.

BILL GOLDSWORTHY

The late Bill Goldsworthy, a tall right winger, played 14 seasons in the NHL. He joined the Boston Bruins for a pair of games late in the 1964–65 season. Used sparingly by Boston, he was claimed by Minnesota in the 1967 Expansion Draft. He blossomed as a North Star and was a fan favorite for the next 10 seasons, eventually having his jersey number retired. His final 2 seasons were spent with the New York Rangers. Goldsworthy amassed 283 goals and 541 points in 771 career games.

"Our dad made many wonderful friends in Minnesota and through-out hockey. Many of them stayed with him throughout his fight," said Tammy and Sean Goldsworthy, Bill's children. "And he always spoke fondly of the players who were his teammates on Team

RIGHT WING
Games played – 3
9
Goals – 1
Assists – 1
Points – 2
PIM – 4

Canada 1972. Playing on that team was the highlight of his career."

Goldsworthy and his wife, June, divorced 15 years prior to his death.

As a Team Canada member, Goldsworthy is remembered for taking two costly first period penalties in game four in Vancouver. The penalties led to a pair of Soviet power play goals and brought on a chorus of boos and jeers directed at Team Canada throughout the game, a 5–3 loss. Goldsworthy said after the game, "I couldn't believe how the fans turned on us. I'm ashamed to be a Canadian."

He scored his only goal of the series during that game.

Goldsworthy in Moscow, checking his stick at practice.

Goldsworthy in discussion with the referee at the Russian net, Toronto.

JOCELYN GUEVREMONT

Jocelyn Guevremont, a Montreal native, was Vancouver's first choice (third overall) in the 1971 Amateur Draft. Having played only 75 NHL games, he was a surprise choice for Team Canada in 1972. On October 14, 1974, he was traded from the Canucks to Buffalo, where he performed for five seasons. He finished his career with the New York Rangers in 1979–80. He played in 571 NHL games, scoring 84 goals and garnering 307 points.

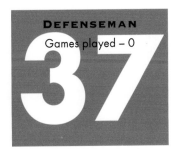

There's no doubt the best memory (of Team Canada '72) would be the phone call that I got, I think it was in July, inviting me to go to the camp. I was just 21 years old at that time, a first-year NHLer, so it was a privilege to be chosen. I know that each team had to be represented by at least two players, so that was one of the reasons why Dale Tallon and I got picked from Vancouver. Overall, it was a great experience.

Mind you, I don't know how seriously we took this whole thing but I think we came back to reality very quickly after the first couple of games. There were about 7 or 10 guys who were on the team but we were never really part of it. We used to call ourselves the Cheerleader Squad, but that was okay. We were all rookies at that time — I'm talking about Marcel Dionne and Dale Tallon and Gilbert Perreault and Rick Martin and me and a few other guys — so it was just a great experience to be there. We weren't really close to Eagleson and Ferguson and Sinden.

In my first day at training camp, I walked in the room where Ferguson and Sinden were, and they shook my hand and their words were, "We don't really want you here, but you're going to be here so just get along with everybody and have a good time." They will never admit they said that to me, but I know they did. At that time, I didn't realize what was going on so it didn't really get to me until later. So that's what I did. I just went along for the ride. I kept my mouth shut and worked hard in all the practices and I was having a ball. At least I can say one thing — they were straight to the point and very honest with me. For me to be on the ice every day with White and Stapleton and Savard and Lapointe and Park was a great experience. They were all the best defensemen in the league at that time, so for me it was awesome just to be there in practice every day.

For me to be on the ice every day with White and Stapleton and Savard and Lapointe and Park was a great experience. They were all the best defensemen in the league at that time, so for me it was awesome just to be there in practice every day.

After the Montreal and Toronto games, there were a couple of us, we'd follow those guys – the Russians – and I couldn't believe the way they could drink beers and vodka...it was unbelievable! How could they stand up on their feet and sing and dance at three o'clock in the morning and have to get up at six to go around the ice for two hours?

I remember the first couple of games in Montreal and in Toronto. After the game, there were a couple of us, we'd follow those guys – the Russians – and I couldn't believe the way they could drink beers and vodka... it was unbelievable! How could they stand up on their feet and sing and dance at three o'clock in the morning and have to get up at six to go around the ice for two hours? I thought, "These guys must be in such great physical condition." But then again, I realized that drinking vodka to them was like drinking Pepsi Cola to us. I have one shot of straight vodka and I pass out.

One big disappointment, and I think it still is recalled today because he won't come to any of the events, is the fact that Gilbert Perreault didn't play much, except for two games and in those games, he dominated the 60 minutes. In Winnipeg, he dominated the whole game and the Russians were actually happy to see him sitting out. Why they decided not to play him we'll probably never know, but to me, that was a major disappointment that he didn't get to play more. I know that's the reason he left Russia that morning and he's still bitter about it 30 years later. I don't think he's ever been to any of the events that Team Canada '72 has held in the past 20 years.

The Russian team had some excellent hockey players, like Yakushev and Kharlamov, and they had some very, very strong defensemen. On our part, by the time we woke up we were already in the third game of the series. You can always say about these guys that they took the bull by the horns and they went to work. Fortunately, it paid off.

The trip, by itself, was the highlight of my life because I'm not a big traveler. I'm a "stay at home" boy. I've been down in Florida for seven years now so even a trip to the beach to me is no great deal. But I remember we had a great time in Sweden. The little time that I spent in Russia, we went to see some of the culture and it was interesting. But I was so young that I didn't really realize what these things were all about.

I came back before the series ended. Sinden never bought my story about me wanting to come back because my wife was sick. That's the only reason I came back. She had been sick from day one, and the doctors on the team wouldn't even take the time to go and see her, and that really pissed me off. They were too busy looking after I don't know what. I know we had some injuries on the team but they could have at least taken 15 minutes to have a look at her. She hadn't eaten in three days and every time she'd eat something, she would throw up.

I didn't know that Gilbert Perreault and Rick Martin were about to leave, too. Sinden and Ferguson thought we were all plotting together because I was friends with Rick and Gilbert, but the only reason, and I'm going to say it again 30 years later, the only reason I came back was because my wife was sick.

Regardless of what happened at the end, when I left the team and came home early, I'm happy today that I can still be a part of all the festivities that they've been holding over the years. It was fun then and it's still fun. It's a memory for the

One big disappointment is the fact that Gilbert Perreault didn't play much, except for two games and in those games, he dominated the 60 minutes. In Winnipeg, he dominated the whole game and the Russians were actually happy to see him sitting out.

Gilbert Perreault heads off Vladimir Vikulov before he causes Tony Esposito trouble.

whole country and I think it was a wake-up call for hockey at the same time. It was a great eye-opener for North Americans. Suddenly we realized we aren't alone in this world — there are other people playing hockey on this planet.

I went on to play eight more seasons in the NHL. I was traded to Buffalo in 1974 and wound up my career in 1980 after a season with the New York Rangers and their New Haven farm team.

After retiring, I went back to Laval. I did a little coaching — I coached midget AAA for one year and then junior major for three years. I was the first Drummondville Voltigers coach in 1982, then I coached in Cornwall for two years, where I had Doug Gilmour and Ray Sheppard on my team.

People don't realize that when you spend almost 10 years in the NHL from the age of 20 to 30, for other people those years are for building their careers. But for most players, our careers are over by age 30, and we've got to start all over again. It's very difficult. I can't speak for everyone, but it was very, very difficult for me. I had serious marital problems at that time and within two years, the whole world collapsed on me. I went bankrupt and I was divorced. So from September 1980 for the next year and a half, the whole world was hell for me. I had managed to save some money during my career, but within eight months of quitting, a "friend" of mine took me to the cleaners. When you're driving two cars and you have a nice house and a cottage up north and you're living the good life, and suddenly you're down to nothing, rock bottom, it hits you pretty hard. I remember the day like it was yesterday when the bank told me I had to foreclose on the house. At that time, a lawyer friend gave me the worst advice that I could get. He told me to declare bankruptcy, which I did, and that's when I began living a life of hell.

In 1984, I was helping Bob Sirois and Yvan Cournoyer in Montreal with the Roadrunners roller-hockey team. During that summer, I met the owner of that team in Miami. I went down and got a job with a hotel. I figured if I had to look for work, I might as well do it where it was warm and I could go to the beach.

Today, I teach hockey in South Florida with Professional Hockey Development. We do hockey clinics and hockey schools. Now I'm getting into a new venture with a football player agent, and we just got our license to become player agents in the NHL. That's going to keep me busy. I know it's going to be tough for the first few years because unless you're lucky and you get an active player,

Jocelyn Guevremont signing memorabilia at the Royal York Hotel, Toronto.

you have to recruit kids 15, 16 years old. By the time they turn pro – if they ever turn pro – it'll take four or five years.

We're going to start another business which will get endorsements for players. You see all the football and baseball and basketball players on TV getting big endorsement contracts and you rarely see the hockey players involved. We hope to change that. Hockey's getting so popular now everywhere in the States that I think the timing is very good.

It's a memory for the whole country and I think it was a wake-up call for hockey at the same time. It was a great eye-opener for North Americans. Suddenly we realized we aren't alone in this world – there are other people playing hockey on this planet.

VIC HADFIELD

Vic Hadfield became the first 50-goal scorer in New York Ranger history in 1971–72, while playing left wing on the famous GAG (goal a game) line. He was also named team captain that season. The Oakville, Ontario, native joined the Rangers in 1961–62 and was traded to Pittsburgh late in his 16-year career. He amassed career totals of 1,002 games, 323 goals, 389 assists and 712 points.

I suppose everyone still remembers me as the player who quit on Team Canada, the player who left Moscow before the end of the series and returned to training camp with the New York Rangers. When I came back I took a surprising amount of heat, even from the local press and the Oakville newspaper. But there was a lot more to it than most people know. Most people don't know that 13 of us from Team Canada were going to come back from Moscow. The news of our departure was supposed to be announced at a press conference. Our services were no longer required so we weren't going to be able to practice and weren't going to be playing any of the remaining games. Alan Eagleson agreed to hold a press conference and explain this to everybody. But he never did it.

In my particular case, I had just signed a five-year contract with the Rangers and training camp was about to start. So I thought if I wasn't going to play in any more games, and more importantly was not going to get any practices in, it was wiser to head home. Thirteen of us decided that we should all come back and head off to our respective NHL training camps.

LEFT WING

11

Games played – 2
Goals – 0
Assists – 0
Points – 0
PIM – 0

Most of the other Team Canada players agreed later that the situation was not handled very well. Most said they had no resentment toward us at the time because they understood all 13 of us had training camps to attend. It was clear that we weren't going to get much ice time in Moscow so the players who stayed really didn't blame us.

That was important to hear, and I have spoken to all the players many times. They could see what was happening and later what turned a lot of the guys off was how Eagleson ran the show. If you weren't a client of his, too bad. He would really not have anything to do with you. And if he could make it rough on you he would not hesitate to do so. I did not like the man. Later on, everyone learned what the situation was. When we left, Eagleson did not fulfill his part of the deal by calling a press conference. I think that would have

I'm still in touch with everybody on Team Canada. We're all still very tight as friends, and I'm glad the guys don't treat me any differently because I left. I certainly am proud of being part of it and pleased they all seem to understand.

As for the series, we were all naturally shocked at the quality of play that the Russian team displayed in that first game in Montreal. I don't think we took them for granted. Because we had never seen them play before, we relied on the scouting reports that we were given. And they turned out to be very misleading and inaccurate.

Anatoli Tarasov, center, the coach of the Central Army team for many years and founding spirit of Soviet hockey, sits in the stands with Vladislav Tretiak. Tarasov was bumped as coach in favor of Bobrov just six months before the series.

been the proper thing to do, it would have helped to explain our reasons for leaving.

Today, years later, we all know how his career turned out but his attitude in Moscow was an indicator of what kind of a guy he was. The final straw for me was attending a practice session and Harry Sinden calling about eight forward lines together and I was left out. I was left standing by the boards. That's the way it was handled and of course it was very humiliating. The coaches then named the players, their final choices, and 13 of us were left to hang out by the boards. We all knew that if we were not chosen it meant we were not going to be playing in any more games and we weren't even going to be able to practice.

So we all decided to leave together, all 13 of us, including Stan Mikita. But Mikita asked for a chance to play in our final match, an exhibition game in Czechoslovakia. And his request was granted. There he would have an opportunity to see his birth parents and other relatives in Prague and he would be named team captain for that

game. So he changed his mind and stayed. That left 10 or 11 of us who were all going to leave together. We had arranged for a bus to take us to the airport in Moscow, but when the bus arrived, only 3 of us showed up. The others had changed their minds. They had decided, or were persuaded, to stay in Russia and have a bit of a holiday. They talked to their wives and I think most of them wanted to stay and enjoy the rest of their time in Russia. Because I had just signed a new contract, I felt very obligated to the Rangers. I thought it was important for me to get ready for the new season. And then all hell broke loose when I left. After that, all I could do was deal with the situation as best I could.

As for the series, we were all naturally shocked at the quality of play that the Russian team displayed in that first game in Montreal. I don't think we took them for granted. Because we had never seen them play before, we relied on the scouting reports that we were given. And they turned out to be very misleading and inaccurate. From the reports, it didn't look like the Russians were going to give us too many problems, but somebody screwed up.

So they hit us hard, really surprised us in Montreal, and we kind of reeled after that first game and bounced back a little bit in the second one. But you could see what was happening as we traveled across Canada. The series began creating a tremendous amount of team spirit in us because we all just felt, "Well, here we are guys, we'd better stick together because it doesn't look like we're going to get too much support as we go across Canada."

I played in that game in Vancouver, where the fans really came down on us and Phil had to make that unforgettable speech. It was a funny kind of a feeling out there and I'm sure we all felt it. I know I'll never forget it. I was thinking, here we are, we gave up a good part of our summer to represent Canada and we were awfully proud of being able to do that. Yet as we went along we just didn't seem to have much support, and that caused the guys to stick together much closer than they might have otherwise.

Fortunately, the team rallied and went on to win the series and I really do think that it was because of the situation we found ourselves in, a situation not of our choice, nor to our liking, but it certainly brought the guys together and there was just no way that we were going to be defeated.

That summer I had to hire someone to look after my golf course business for me. Other guys had hockey schools or some kind of other off-season employment back then. We were all promised quite a lump sum amount of money if we won the series and it was supposed to go into our pension plans. But whether it ever went in or not nobody

seems to know, especially with all the avenues that Eagleson controlled to put the money away. But we did get a little something. As I recall, we were given $1,500 dollars, which wasn't much. I turned my share over to a charity in New York.

When we went over to play in Sweden, all of the players had problems with the Swedes, especially Wayne Cashman. But I had my problems too with Lars Erik Sjoberg, who later played with the Winnipeg Jets. He was Sweden's Player of the Year in '69. Sjoberg liked to clip me from behind or spear me in the back of my skate to make me fall backward. He did this to me a couple of times, until I got so mad I had to rearrange his face to make him realize that he shouldn't be doing that. He got the message and a photo of his bloody face was in all the papers. And then someone speared Cashman right in the mouth. Cash had a dreadful wound on the inside of his mouth. That was the same night there was a bomb threat back at the hotel. So we weren't allowed back into our hotel that night.

Because of the rough play in those games, the Canadian ambassador in Sweden didn't give us much support and even one of our team doctors, Jim Murray, turned on us until somebody told him to shove off. There was plenty of tension during that phase of the series. But again, it was the guys who put the skates on who held the team together and we just stayed together as a unit, trying to ignore all of the bullshit that was coming our way. Looking back, I don't think there are too many teams that would have tolerated all the bullshit we received. But it only made us more determined to do well.

The day we landed in Russia, we came out of the airport and loaded onto the bus and suddenly they couldn't find the bus driver. So we had to wait for

Hadfield races around a downed Don Awrey, trying to beat out Vladimir Shadrin.

I played in that game in Vancouver, where the fans really came down on us and Phil had to make that unforgettable speech. It was a funny kind of a feeling out there and I'm sure we all felt it. I know I'll never forget it. I was thinking, here we are, we gave up a good part of our summer to represent Canada and we were awfully proud of being able to do that.

this guy for a good hour. I think that was a tactic they used deliberately, to annoy us and to try to throw us off our game. Then when we got to the hotel they assigned two or three guys in one room with one bed. The next day they took all of our food and our beer went missing. That really ticked us off.

A lot of bullshit came from the Eagleson group. But I also felt that Harry Sinden could have been stronger. He could have been a little more aggressive in sticking up for the players, who were often frustrated. But he was so tight with Eagleson that his loyalties were divided.

I loved John Ferguson. I never had a problem with him, still don't today. I fully respect him. He was an assistant coach and naturally he had to do what he was told. And he didn't have any real say as to who would play and who would not. I don't think Fergie made any of the major decisions. Everything was controlled by Eagleson and his group. All the stuff that's come out since then about his methods and morality really backs up anything

I've got to say. You could see it all the way across Canada, all the political bullshit, simple things like not being able to get tickets for friends because they'd all been distributed elsewhere.

When I got home and saw that even my local paper was cutting me up for leaving, it was very difficult to deal with. I knew deep down that I had done the right thing and so did the other young players who left to attend their training camps. Because they were younger than I was, they escaped a lot of the flak. I was there to receive most of the blunt criticism. But it was my choice to leave and it was the right choice. Ranger General Manager Emile Francis helped me by getting the media to listen to my side of the story. People must have listened because shortly after that I started getting fan mail, and 9 out of every 10 writers said they now had a better understanding of what had taken place over there. And they commended me for my actions. I answered every one of those fan letters. And with all the problems that Eagleson later ran into, they certainly gained a better perspective of him as well.

Even in the final game, when Eagleson went across the ice with his middle finger standing up, everyone knew that was just disgraceful. It was boorish. When you see that image broadcast throughout the world, your Team Canada leader representing Canada in such a manner, and then laughing it off and saying he was trying to show we're number one, that was shameful. The man could have been a great figure in hockey and he blew it all because of his greed. Back then he was a powerful figure, and if he had used his head, he may have done wonderful things for the game we all love. But even the guys that stayed over there — like Brad Park, Marcel Dionne, Stan Mikita — all of those guys became very critical of him. Now they have a much better understanding of Eagleson and of why we came home. If he'd only held that press conference like he promised there would have been no confusion and no blame.

I think he didn't say anything because he had a dislike for me. And he knew I didn't care much for him. I think he was looking for a way out if the team ever lost the series. Then he had somebody — the deserters — to blame. There wasn't a bigger booster for the team than me and the other two guys who came home. We were keenly interested in what was happening over in Moscow. We knew the team was going to do well. We never for a minute thought that we had done the wrong thing.

Of course, it's unfortunate that I was deprived of the glory that went along with that eighth-game victory. But I made my choice and I knew I wasn't going to be contributing on the ice. I knew Harry was going to stick with his 18 guys, which I thought was fine. He selected a lot of tremendous players and I didn't feel that I was any better or any worse than any one of them. Being left off the final roster wasn't the problem. It was when we couldn't practice, and the way it was handled, that bothered me.

I'm still in touch with everybody on Team Canada. We're all still very tight as friends, and I'm glad the guys don't treat me any differently because I left. I certainly am proud of being part of it and pleased they all seem to understand.

After the series, and after I retired from the NHL in 1977 with over 1,000 games as a Ranger

Vic Hadfield at the Hockey Hall of Fame.

and Penguin under my belt, I got into the golf business. These days I run the Vic Hadfield Golf Center in Woodbridge, Ontario. And I still do a lot of work in New York so I'm back and forth quite a bit. I represent a computer firm in New York and I have my own foundation for a family there — it's for leukemia research and this will be our fourth year. We raised about half a million dollars that goes toward finding a cure for the disease. I started working with this family affected by leukemia because it provided an opportunity to really be involved in something this large and this important. Every cent that we net goes right into research. I get a tremendous amount of satisfaction out of doing this work. Someday soon, through our efforts and others, we hope to see this terrible disease defeated.

SOVIET UNION

Game 5: September 22, 1972

Luzhniki Sports Palace, Moscow

Stopping in Sweden for two exhibition games to get used to the larger European ice, the Canadian team was still struggling to find its identity. Three thousand Canadian faithful made the arduous trip to watch their team fight back to take the series. As well, 10,000 telegrams of support greeted Team Canada when it arrived in Moscow. The players were feeling rejuvenated.

For the fourth time in five games, Canada scored first, with Parise taking a Perreault pass all the way.

That would be all the scoring in the first period, which was followed in the second frame with two more Canadian goals, one from Clarke with an assist from Henderson and another from Henderson with assists from Clarke and Lapointe.

Leading 3–0 at the start of the third period, then 3–1, the wheels fell off when the Soviets scored four unanswered goals, two of them separated by only eight seconds, staking the Russians to a 5–4 victory.

Little did anyone know that night that the Henderson myth was about to be born. Crashing heavily into the boards and suffering a likely concussion, he ignored doctors' advice to sit things out. Not only did he stay in the game but he scored a second time that night – on his very next shift after the accident. Amazing yes, but only a shadow of what was to come.

Stats

USSR 5, Canada 4
Attendance: 15,000.

FIRST PERIOD
1. Canada, Parise (Perreault, Gilbert) 15:30.
Penalties: Ellis 3:49; Kharlamov 12:25.

SECOND PERIOD
2. Canada, Clarke (Henderson) 2:36.
3. Canada, Henderson (Lapointe, Clarke) 11:47.
Penalties: Ellis and Kharlamov 5:38; Bergman 8:13; Blinov and White 20:00.

THIRD PERIOD
4. USSR, Blinov (Petrov, Kuzkin) 3:34.
5. Canada, Henderson (Clarke) 4:56.
6. USSR, Anisin (Liapkin, Yakushev) 9:05.
7. USSR, Shadrin (Anisin) 9:13.
8. USSR, Gusev (Ragulin, Kharlamov) 11:41.
9. USSR, Vikulov (Kharlamov) 14:46.
Penalties: Clarke and Tsigankov 10:25.

SHOTS ON GOAL
Canada: 12-13-12 – 37
USSR: 9-13-11 – 33
Goalies: Canada, T. Esposito; USSR, Tretiak.

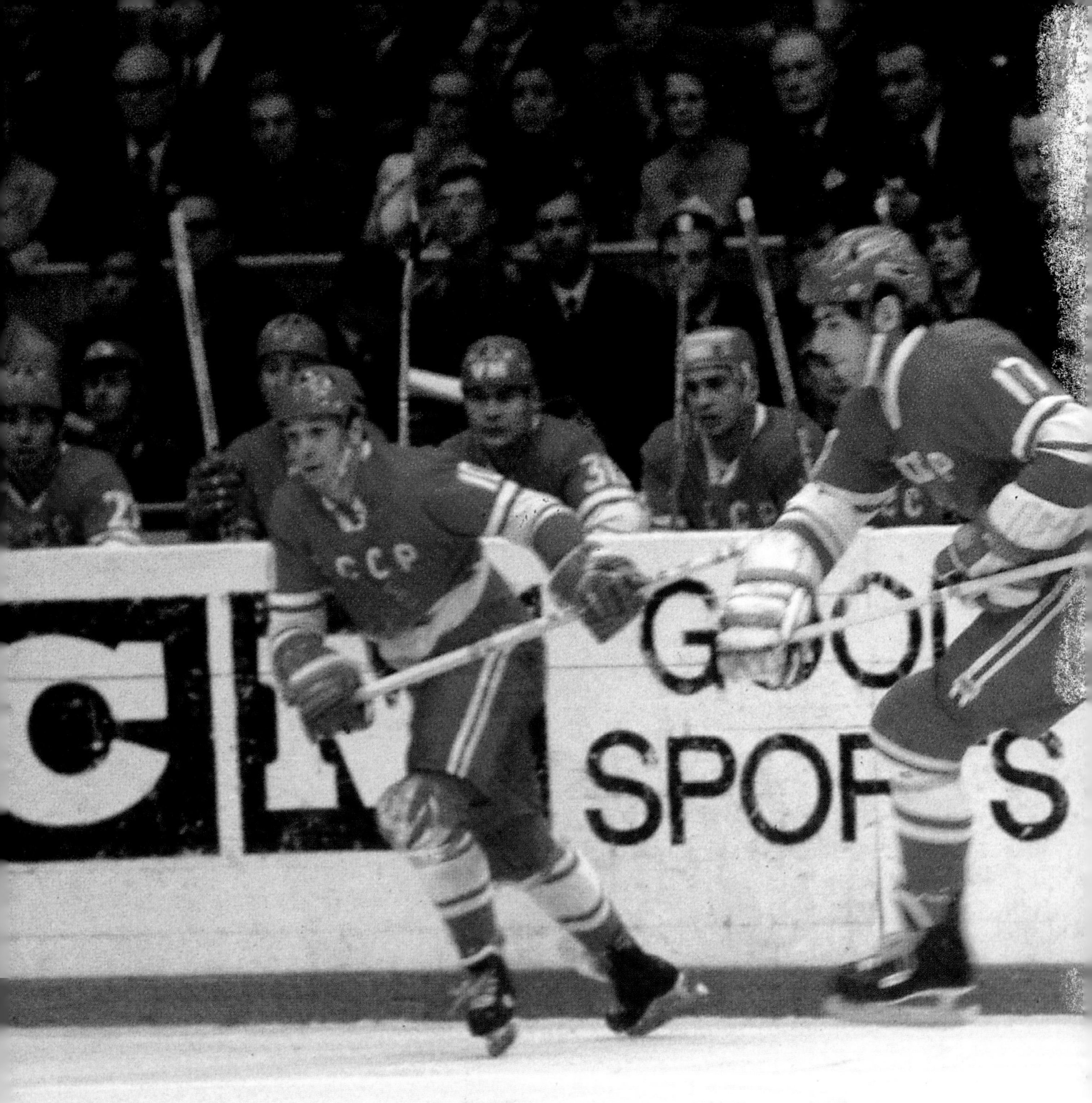
СССР

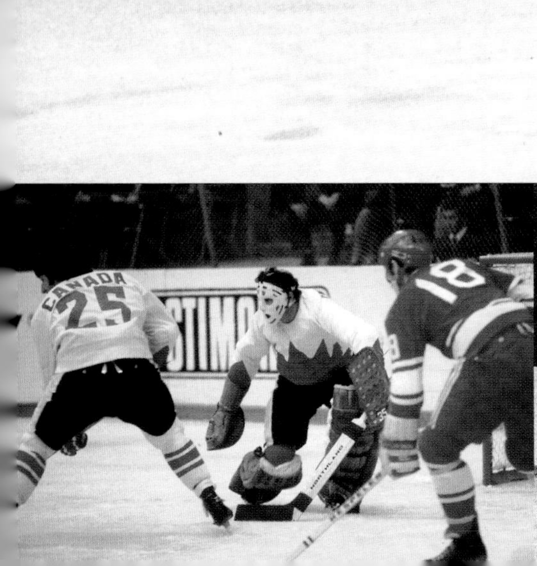
CANADA
25
18

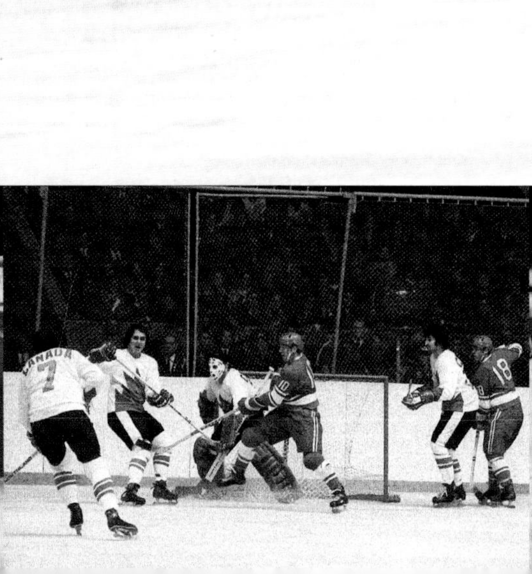
CANADA
7
18

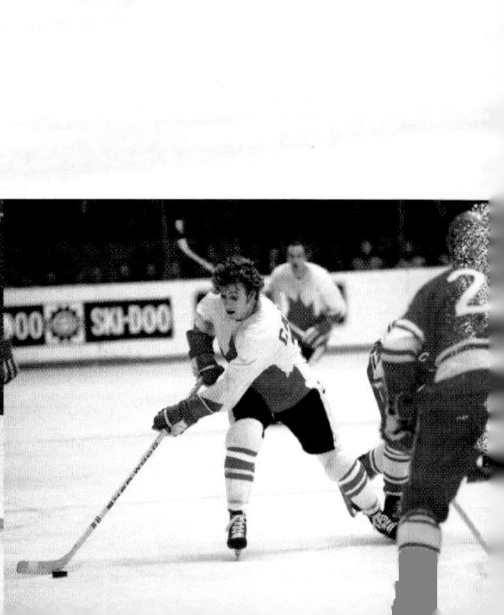
SKI-DOO

Game 6: September 24, 1972

Luzhniki Sports Palace, Moscow

Despite a seriously suspicious penalty differential of 31 minutes to 4 in favor of the Soviets, the Canadians pulled off a 3–2 win. With Russia scoring first just over a minute into the second period, Canada's awe-inspiring comeback started with a flurry of three goals in only 83 seconds. Dennis Hull, Yvan Cournoyer and Paul Henderson combined to beat not only the Soviet team but the officials as well.

Inexperienced German officials called an odd assortment of penalties, seeming to notice only Canada's indiscretions, although a famous missed goal call could have tied the game for Russia. Ken Dryden was able to pull back a puck from five inches inside the goal line when it hit the extra mesh that the Soviets hang in the net to stop pucks from bouncing out.

This was the night Henderson scored his first game-winner. It was a feat he would perform each night until the end of the series.

Stats

Canada 3, USSR 2
Attendance: 15,000.

FIRST PERIOD
No scoring.
Penalties: Bergman 10:21; P. Esposito 13:11.

SECOND PERIOD
1. USSR, Liapkin (Yakushev) 1:12.
2. Canada, Hull 5:13.
3. Canada, Cournoyer (Berenson) 6:31.
4. Canada, Henderson 6:36.
5. USSR, Yakushev (Shadrin) 17:11.
Penalties: Ragulin 2:09; Lapointe and Vasiliev 8:29; Clarke (minor and misconduct) 10:12; Hull 17:02; P. Esposito (major) 17:46; Canada interfering with referee 17:46.

THIRD PERIOD
No scoring.
Penalties: Ellis 17:31.

SHOTS ON GOAL
Canada: 7-8-7 – 22
USSR: 12-8-9 – 29
Goalies: Canada, Dryden; USSR, Tretiak.

PAUL HENDERSON

Paul Henderson gained everlasting fame when he poked his own rebound past Vladimir Tretiak in the final seconds of game eight in the Summit Series of 1972. He was a key figure in a 1968 multiplayer trade that brought him to Toronto from Detroit and sent Frank Mahovlich to the Red Wings. Unhappy with Leaf owner Harold Ballard, Henderson skipped to the Toronto Toros of the WHA and moved to Birmingham when the Toros relocated to Alabama in 1973–74. Henderson played one final season with Atlanta in the NHL in 1979–80.

Often at sports dinners and on other occasions, I tell people, "I'm the only guy who played pro hockey for 18 seasons and scored just one lousy goal." It usually draws a laugh.

Still, it was a goal that people can't forget. Almost every day of every week they want to talk to me about it. They want to tell me where they were and what they were doing when I scored it. They want to shake my hand. Today it happened at a hotel. Yesterday it happened a couple of times at a golf tournament. A lady rushed over and said, "Mr. Henderson, I've got to have your autograph. I think your goal meant more to my husband than when our children were born." And for me to discuss the goal, well, it's become a part of my life. It's become a very common occurrence ever since September 1972. Oddly enough, it seems to be intensifying. Every year there seems to be more interest in that goal than ever before. Don't ask me why.

How has it affected my life? Well, obviously that goal in '72 has endeared me in the hearts of Canadians and given me a small niche in the psyches of Canadians. I am, and forever will be, identified with that goal, even though – and this may surprise

RIGHT WING
Games played – 8
Goals – 7
Assists – 3
Points – 10
PIM – 4

19

you – it may not compare with some of the other blessings I've been granted in my life.

Obviously the spiritual dimensions of my life have perhaps given me a different perspective on such things as game-winning goals and allowed me to understand how fortunate I am, not to be just "Paul Henderson, the goal-scorer" who, at 29, helped win a long-ago memorable series. I'm thankful to be blessed with other attributes, and hopefully I've been able to make a few other worthy contributions to my fellow Canadians, too.

First, just to be born in Canada has been a blessing. To be married to a wonderful woman, Eleanor [nee Alton], for over 30 years, to have three married daughters and five grandchildren are other blessings I cherish. To have good health is yet another.

So you can see that scoring "The Goal," while high on the list, is not the most important thing that ever happened to me. But I must admit it was a great feeling to be in the right place at the right time, and to put that winner in the net.

Paul Henderson came through with the winning goal. He rushed in alone on two Russian defenders and beat them both. He pushed the puck around one, then picked it up again and beat the next guy. Even though he was hit and knocked off balance, while falling he fired a shot under Tretiak's arm for what turned out to be the game-winner. Even though he scored a more famous one in game eight, that goal by Henderson assured us of a chance to win the series. It was a spectacular play and one of the most remarkable goals I ever saw." – *Gary Bergman on game seven*

Henderson breaks free of the Soviets with Bobby Clarke ready in the wings.

Some people say, "Paul, what a shame you haven't been inducted into the Hockey Hall of Fame." And I reply, "Listen, the worst thing they could do to me is put me in the Hall of Fame. They do that and everybody will forget about me."

Seriously, they have a selection committee for the Hall of Fame and I understand the predicament they're in. You don't put a man in the Hall without serious thought. Some of the people in the Hall I wouldn't have selected. Others who aren't in the Hall I would like to see in there. But it's not my call.

Am I upset with the selection committee? No, of course I'm not. They have a job to do – a tough job. Whether I ever get in or not isn't really going to affect who Paul Henderson really is.

He shot once and shot again. The light flashed. I was right behind Paul when he scored the goal. If I'd had a camera, I could have taken the nicest shot of him. But he would have knocked the camera from my hands because that's when he jumped into my arms and we began celebrating. – *Yvan Cournoyer*

Vladislav Tretiak came to know Henderson as an extremely deadly competitor.

As for my memories of '72? Oh boy, I remember thinking early in game one, even though we'd jumped into a 2–0 lead, that the Soviets had a great team and we would have our hands full. Then there was the sinking feeling in the pit of my stomach a few minutes later, when the Russians roared back to erase our 2–0 lead.

I remember Pete Mahovlich's goal in game two. It was an absolutely incredible goal, and short-handed, too. It was the highlight goal in a much-needed win. I remember Phil Esposito clumping back into the dressing room after game four, a disappointing loss in Vancouver, and he said, "Well, I just told the Canadian people off." That speech of Phil's was a very significant factor in the series. It proved to me and to everyone else that Phil was a great leader.

I remember game five in Moscow and how I scored a pair of goals and after 40 minutes we were leading 3–0. Ron Ellis had done a superb job of checking Valeri Kharlamov. Then, in a six-minute span in the third, the Russians scored five times and beat us 5–4. I remember thinking we were still going to win the series, even after that bitter defeat.

I remember scoring the winning goals in games six and seven and while everyone talks about the goal I scored to win game eight, I call the game seven winner absolutely the best goal I ever scored in my life. It was a one on two situation – me against two Soviet defensemen. Somehow I slipped by them both – something I didn't do that often – and I scored on Tretiak.

I remember the final game, with 20 minutes to play, and Team Canada trailing 5–3. And, despite the deficit, how everyone in the dressing room was confident and upbeat. The thought of losing didn't cross any of our minds. In the final seconds of that game, I stood up at the bench and called Pete Mahovlich off the ice. I'd never done such a thing before. I jumped on and rushed straight for their net. I had this strange feeling that I could score the winning goal. I had a great chance just before I scored, but Cournoyer's pass went behind me. Then I was tripped up and crashed into the boards behind the net. I leaped up and moved in front, just in time to see Esposito take a shot at Tretiak from inside the faceoff circle. The rebound came right to my stick and I tried to slide the puck past Tretiak. Damn! He got a piece of it. But a second rebound came right to me. This time I flipped the puck over him and into the net.

There was instant elation. Cournoyer was the first player to reach me and embrace me. Then all the players were there. And I remember thinking of my dad who had passed away in 1968. I remember wishing he could have been there to see that goal. The final 34 seconds ticked away and we'd won the most grueling, up-and-down series any of us had ever played in.

The Russians had such a cohesive team. I'd never played against a team like that before. They had a game plan and they had players with a multitude of skills. In Winnipeg, they decided to go with

Henderson and Bobby Clarke digging for rebounds, Toronto.

their kid line and we felt we'd show these young Russian kids a thing or two. Well, that line beat the snot out of us.

Playing on Team Canada was a wonderful opportunity for me. Had they picked only 20 or 22 players Paul Henderson would not have been invited to camp. But when it went to 35 players I really felt that I would get invited. And thank goodness that I was.

My good buddy Ron Ellis was also invited because we had played on a line together in Toronto. In camp there were seven lines made up of 21 forwards. At best we thought we would be fourth line. There were a lot of centermen selected but when they picked this kid Bobby Clarke from the Flyers, it caused a lot of controversy. A lot of people wanted to know why they passed on Dave Keon or Norm Ullman or Pit Martin.

So Ellis and I decided the one centerman we didn't want was Bobby Clarke. Then they would probably be looking at us as the seventh line. We went to camp and on the first day they put down the lines – Henderson, Ellis and Clarke. Clarke was

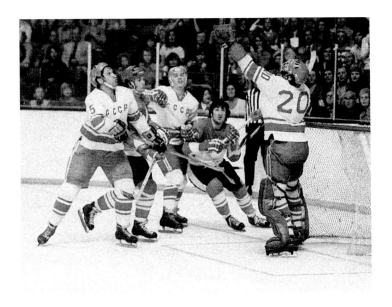

I remember scoring the winning goals in games six and seven and while everyone talks about the goal I scored to win game eight, I call the game seven winner absolutely the best goal I ever scored in my life.

Henderson and Guy Lapointe pressure Vladislav Tretiak to catch an airborne puck, Montreal.

not a household name then. But Harry Sinden and John Ferguson put the three of us together and we decided, it looks like we're the underdogs so let's give it our best shot and see if we can crack this lineup.

Bobby Clarke turned out to be one of the most dedicated hockey players that ever played the game. The best thing that could have happened to Ronnie and me was to get this young kid making plays for us. He was terrific. We were the only line that played together in all eight games in that series. And the media began calling us Canada's best line. We were put together as a checking line and ended up scoring a lot of goals along the way. It was a tremendous experience, it really was. When we went over to Russia, not only did we shut them down, I scored the winning goals in the sixth, seventh and eighth games.

When I came back to Canada I was placed on a pedestal by the whole country. It was incredible. They gave me a car and golf clubs. I was asked to appear on this program and that program, and everybody in the world wanted my autograph. I was at a stoplight one day and a guy in the car two lanes over recognizes me. He gets out of his

car and runs over and says, "I want your autograph." I said, "There's guys behind us." The light changed and guys started beeping their horns and he's saying to them, "Shut up, it's Paul Henderson, I'm getting his autograph." I mean it was ridiculous.

I think I'm much more satisfied with some of the other things I've done with my life since 1972. I started a group called Leadership Ministries, beginning with just three men in 1985. Now we have 65 groups of men getting together to discuss the spiritual aspects of life — issues like how to be good husbands and fathers; how to set priorities in life; how to get the most out of life; how to find balance in what we do; and what kind of a legacy will we leave? What will our wives, children, grandchildren — and our friends — say and think about us when we're gone?

So many people have mentored me along the way. A man in Birmingham, Alabama, helped me immensely when I played hockey there — a man named John Bradford, a very astute man, and a very successful businessman.

Bobby Clarke to Henderson in a dominant Canadian play.

I can tell you that scoring that goal in Russia, from an athletic standpoint, was the greatest thing ever to happen to me. But when I compare "the goal of the century," as people have come to call it, to having the Lord as my Savior and walking with Him at my side, even that goal pales into insignificance.

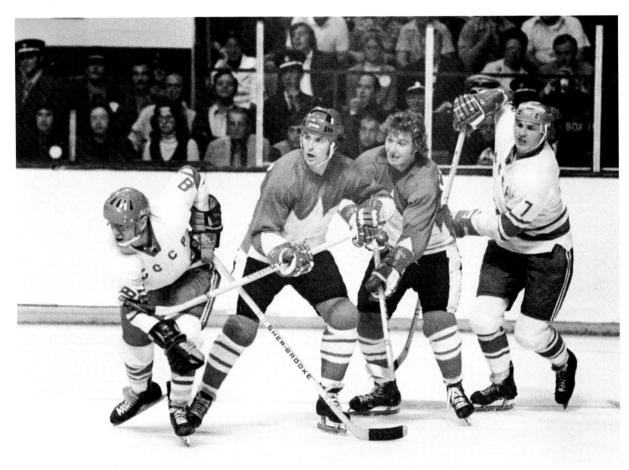

Henderson and Bobby Clarke locked in a duel with Gennady Tsigankov, far right, and Soviet teammate .

In my early years in the NHL, I felt that I had everything I had ever set out in life to accomplish. But deep down there was a restlessness. And I could never seem to be content. I used to talk to people and ask them, "Are you satisfied with where you are?" I started to ask questions like, "What is the real purpose and meaning to life?" and I could never get any solid answers.

Then I met one of these religious guys, one of these born-againers, one of these Christians. His name was Mel Stevens. He was the owner of Teen Ranch north of Toronto, and he was a hockey fan.

Back then I didn't know what born-again meant, and I used to make fun of these religious fanatics.

But this man Stevens started to ask me some questions that really got me thinking. He'd say, "Paul, if you died tonight, do you know where you'd spend eternity?" Well, I was only 28 and eternity, what was that all about? I thought Christianity was for people who couldn't cut it, for people who needed a crutch. Then you might turn to God. But a man's man certainly didn't need any God to get him through. So I was somewhat negative toward Mel Stevens at first.

Even so, I realized that I had worries and fears that troubled me. Real fears, like a fear of dying young. And feelings of anger and bitterness. I realized I was furious with the man who controlled my hockey life – Leaf owner Harold Ballard. I was disturbed by the way he acted and I resented the way he treated his players.

Paul Henderson has a busy and fulfilling post-hockey life.

Then I asked my wife, "Do you think there is anything after all of this?" And we weren't really sure. Fortunately we grew up going to Sunday school and church, and we heard the stories from the Bible. But I had set all that aside. I was going to be a man's man. And there were no Mike Gartners, Laurie Boshmans, Ryan Walters, Keith Browns, Pinball Clemens or Joe Carters around – none of these Christian athletes. I didn't know any. In fact, I didn't think you even could be a hockey player and Christian at the same time. So I was a little negative.

But I started to look into it. I got a Bible. I read it once and for the next few months I drove Mel Stevens crazy, asking thousands of questions. I read the Bible through several times and I tried to look at the whole spectrum. And I came to believe that there was a God in Heaven who loved me very much, who didn't want me to be discontented or disturbed or restless, who wanted my life to have purpose and meaning. I believe that I had become separated from God because of things I had done earlier in my life. I had basically said, "God, you go your way and I'll go mine." Paul Henderson did everything he wanted to do, when he wanted to do it. And believe me, professional athletes with acclaim and money have an opportunity to lead fast-paced, irresponsible lives with seldom a thought for the consequences of their actions. I soon learned from others and from the Bible that the penalty for breaking God's rules and commandments is not a few minutes in the penalty box, soon to be forgotten, but it can be as severe as eternal separation from God. I realized I didn't want that.

I became involved in full-time Christian work in 1984. Today, groups of men in our Leadership Ministries meet in boardrooms early in the morning. We help each other deal with the realities of life. My wife and I also conduct marriage seminars on weekends, which help couples achieve a solid, satisfying marriage. I also do a lot of speaking in Christian circles and I really enjoy doing motivational speaking for corporations.

I can tell you that scoring that goal in Russia, from an athletic standpoint, was the greatest thing ever to happen to me, and playing in over 1,000 games in two pro leagues also makes me proud. But when I compare "the goal of the century," as people have come to call it, to having the Lord as my Savior and walking with Him at my side, even that goal pales into insignificance.

DENNIS HULL

Dennis Hull always played in the shadow of his famous brother, Bobby "The Golden Jet" Hull. Even so, he had 14 productive seasons in the NHL with the Chicago Blackhawks and with Detroit (for his final season) where he scored his 300th career goal. He played in 959 games, scoring 303 goals and 351 assists for 654 points. Today, he is an extremely popular after dinner speaker.

The final game was more than a memory – it was a relief. Where was I when Henderson scored? It's a testament to Harry Sinden's great coaching that I was sitting on the bench. But I was on the ice with about two minutes to play when there was a commercial break for the TV sponsors. I looked up in the stands and saw Leonid Brezhnev, the head of the Soviet government, sitting in a box. Just then he kissed another politician on the cheek as a sign of celebration. I guess he figured a tie would give the series to the Soviets because they had scored one more goal than we had.

I played a few more seconds and then came off, giving way to Phil Esposito, Peter Mahovlich and Yvan Cournoyer. Espo was to finish the game because we wanted him out there. He was our leader. Then Paul Henderson stood up and yelled at Pete to come off. Nobody told Henderson to get out there but Pete heard him and came right to the bench. That sort of thing doesn't happen very often. Then came Henderson's heroics and the game-winning goal. I can't understand why Tretiak didn't stop Henderson's shot. Paul came out in front – he was so alone there – and simply banged away at it and it went in.

LEFT WING
Games played – 4
Goals – 2
Assists – 2
Points – 4
PIM – 4

When Henderson popped that goal, I looked up to where Brezhnev was sitting, and his mood – everybody's mood – had changed completely. There was no kissing then. Boy, did they look sour. Very grim.

When Stan Mikita played in Czechoslovakia in our final exhibition game, I had tears in my eyes. Stan received a 10-minute standing ovation and it was very emotional. And here's how Harry picked the players for that game. We were all hungover so he lined us up and looked us over. "You look all right to play," he'd say to one of us, and, "You'd better sit out," he'd say to another. That's how he got his roster. I must have looked pretty sober so I got to play.

Earlier that week, I was actually thinking of going home with Vic Hadfield and the others. If you weren't going to play in Moscow, it seemed pretty hopeless. But when I stayed, I found a position through attrition because Hadfield and Richard Martin were both left wingers. I was glad I stayed because I got to play with one of the greatest guys I've ever met – Jean Ratelle. He reminded me of Jean Beliveau – classy. He was very good to play with, very encouraging. I played

Hull scouting for a loose puck as Rod Gilbert takes a new position.

with him in Vancouver, where he told me, "Just relax and play your own game." I played with Jean and Rod Gilbert in the last three games of the series. Rod was an outstanding player, too. We just clicked so well that I heard the Rangers tried to trade for me when the series was over. Billy Reay [the Chicago coach] told me they offered Hadfield in exchange.

I thought we played pretty good in Vancouver but Goldsworthy took a couple of penalties early in the game and they scored on us. Then the crowd came down on us pretty hard and Phil went out

and gave them his state-of-the-union speech. We were coming together by then.

Frank Mahovlich had allergy problems in Vancouver and his eyes were swollen shut. On the plane the next day, I asked, "Frank, what happened?" He said, "The Russians caught me after the game last night and beat me up."

I liked Harry Sinden. I remember when we left Sweden for Moscow, he knew we were going to be all right. I said to him, "Harry, we're in tough. We have to win three out of four in Moscow." And he said, "Dennis, when we started out we were just a

A show of force: Hull the offender with the exceptional defense pair of Pat Stapleton and Bill White.

out from our net, he'd pass it! I could never figure out why.

I guess everybody remembers Jean-Paul Parise and how he got thrown out of the final game for threatening to hit the referee. Well, a funny thing happened on the way to Prague after the series was over. The referee was on our flight and he was really afraid. You could see him shaking. And Jean-Paul came down the aisle just as a meal was being served. He walked by and flipped the ref's tray up, dumping food all over him. I guess he figured the ref couldn't throw him out of an airplane. We thought it was hilarious.

Pat Stapleton and Bill White played superbly in Moscow. When people talk about defensemen they talk about individuals – Bobby Orr, Brad Park, Ray Bourque. But working as a pair, there was nobody better than White and Stapleton in Moscow in '72.

Hockey players aren't brain surgeons, right? Well, in Moscow, Patty not only convinced the players there was a great Chinese restaurant in town but he had 15 players sign up for a trip to the Moscow Golf and Country Club.

bunch of players. We're a team now. And we're going to surprise a lot of people."

For the Russians, I thought Yakushev was just fabulous. He looked like Eric Nesterenko with talent. A big right winger, he was right in my face. And he could fly, almost as fast as their other big star, Kharlamov. A great player. He could shoot the puck 100 miles an hour and when he got 20 feet

Marcel Dionne was just a kid in '72 and Patty took him aside shortly after training camp opened. He said, "Marcel, you're going to be my roommate when we get to Moscow but there's a problem. There's such a shortage of beds in Moscow that when the wives and girlfriends come over, it's going to be four people in one bed. So here's what we'll do. I'm married so you can't sleep next to my wife Jackie. So Jackie will sleep on the outside, then I'll be next to her. But I don't want to sleep next to you, so it'll be your girlfriend next and then you."

Marcel said, "But I don't want you sleeping next to my girlfriend." And Patty said Marcel went to Harry and lodged a complaint about this four-in-a-bed situation.

I remember how friendly the people were in Moscow. They were very nice. I especially liked the lady who stood outside our shower in the dressing room. When we came out, she was there to hand us a towel.

Those reports that the Russians phoned us at all hours to throw us off our game was so much bull. It was just that the phone system was so archaic that to phone from one room to another you had to dial 13 numbers. Everybody kept getting wrong numbers.

On the flight home, Bobby Clarke and I decided we'd try to find out how many times we could get Harry Sinden to shake hands. So we'd mill around and then approach him. "Great series, Harry," and we'd shake his hand. A minute later, "Great coaching, Harry," and we'd shake his hand. This happened 15 times before he shouted, "What the hell is going on with you two?"

Then in Montreal, Bobby Clarke and I flanked Prime Minister Trudeau on a fire truck in the parade. Someone had given us stickers with our jersey numbers on them to stick to our baggage. We had a couple of extra stickers in our pockets so I took mine and slapped Trudeau on the back, leaving my number 10 on his suit. Then Bobby did the same. So the Prime Minister is walking around with our team numbers decorating his suit.

Guy Lapointe is a great guy, a funny man. We played a reunion game against the Russians in Ottawa about 10 years ago and Guy kept giving us words of encouragement. After the first period, he said, "You're playin' good, guys, but don' get a swelled head, eh." After the second period he said

Hull at Team Canada training camp, with Peter Mahovlich in the background.

it again: "You're playin' good, guys, but don' get a swelled head, eh." Then he went into the can for a smoke. So I took a screwdriver from the trainer and made his helmet smaller. Well, he came out of the john and said, "Let's go, guys, but don' get a swelled head, eh." Then he jammed his helmet on and he couldn't get it over his ears. Geez, the guys howled at that little scene. Guy knew I'd done it because he pointed at me and said, "You, Dennis, you're a funny son of a bitch, eh."

Billy Reay said something to me before I left for Team Canada's training camp. He said, "I'm happy for you, Dennis, that you're on Team Canada, but you know, when you come back, it will never be the same for you in the NHL." And he was right.

Denis Hull, right, enjoys a laugh with Canadian singer Michael Burgess.

Guys I once had no use for had become my best friends. I couldn't play against them the same way I once did. We all had gained so much respect for each other.

Someone once said to me, "Dennis, if only your brother Bobby had played for Team Canada, and Bobby Orr, the series wouldn't have been so close — or so memorable." And I said, "That's right. The Russians would have won eight straight games." He didn't think it was funny.

I was sitting next to Richard Martin one time. We were signing some Team Canada memorabilia and every time Richard signed, he put a D after his name. I nudged him and said, "Richard, you weren't a defenseman." He said, "No, that stands for deserter."

The more I saw Phil Esposito play in 1972 the more I thought how stupid Chicago was to trade him away. He wouldn't let anybody quit. He became a great team leader and showed the same qualities Bobby Clarke showed in leading the Flyers to the Stanley Cup a couple of years later. Phil was fabulous.

Early in his career, with Chicago, he was a little weak on faceoffs. I remember a faceoff next to our goalie Glenn Hall, and Billy Reay called Phil to the bench. He said, "Phil, after you lose the draw, stay with your man."

It's funny, I asked Yvan Cournoyer after the game if winning in Moscow felt anything like winning the Stanley Cup. He said, "No, Dennis, this is 10 times better." So from then on, despite the fact I never managed to play on a Stanley Cup winner, I've always felt like I played on 10 of them.

I've been very busy since I retired from the NHL. Recently I bought a farm north of Toronto and I had a new barn built on the property. I was the sports director of a small college outside Chicago for a time. And I was involved in a car dealership in the Niagara area. But I'm known more for my speechmaking than anything else, having been booked at hundreds of events over the past 20 years. People seem to enjoy my humor, especially my stories (some of them are even true) about my brother Bobby. People say I laugh harder than anyone else at my own jokes. I tell them, "That's because I never heard most of them before." I also put a lot of those stories in a book called *The Third Best Hull*.

ED JOHNSTON

Ed Johnston, a former Boston Bruin, was the last goaltender to play every minute of every game for his team during a season (1962–63). He was with the Bruins when they won the Stanley Cup in 1970. With 30 wins and only 6 losses, he helped Boston to a record-setting season in 1970–71, then helped them win a second Stanley Cup in 1972. He was traded to Toronto (for Jacques Plante) in 1973, spent one season with the Leafs, three more with the St. Louis Blues and a final season with the Chicago Blackhawks. He left the NHL with 236 career victories and 32 shutouts. Later, as general manager of the Pittsburgh Penguins, he named Mario Lemieux as his team's number one draft choice.

GOALTENDER
Games played – 0

1

Just being on the team was a thrill — just being one of the guys. I remember we went into training camp and I think our scouting reports on the Russians told us they weren't very good, that they were disorganized. We watched a practice one day before we played them and said, "We should kill this team." Fortunately, or unfortunately, we got off to an early lead by a couple of goals in the game, and all of a sudden the alarm clock went off for those guys and they never gave us the puck after that. I don't think we prepared ourselves enough — either mentally or physically — because of that scouting report. We didn't think we'd have much of a problem. We found out in a hurry that we had to get in better shape and get our minds focused on what we had to do.

Kharlamov was just a terrific player for them and they had Tretiak in the net — he was a super goalkeeper. I don't think anybody figured him out in the early part of the series because we'd never seen his style of goaltending before. Overall, their team was very, very strong. It was a high-skill, high-speed team. There weren't too many players on that team who couldn't step right into the NHL and be an impact player in the league. They just had tremendous skills.

Once we got going, Espo stepped it up a little bit after we got beat in Vancouver. He became a leader. Peter Mahovlich, Cournoyer, Bergie [Gary Bergman] — we had a solid club. It was just a matter of applying ourselves. We had the speed — we had

Ed Johnston honored at the Hockey Hall of Fame, Toronto.

Team Canada players were met in Russia by their wives. Marcel Dionne, center, and Bobby Clarke (in white sweater) mid right.

Cournoyer, Henderson with terrific speed, Ronnie Ellis — we had all the tools. We just got caught off-guard a little bit. After we left Montreal, we knew right away that we had to bring a lot more pride to our performance. Every game, I saw us getting a little bit sharper, a little bit better. I felt that after we got on track, they weren't going to beat us.

I was just really pleased to be part of it. I played in a game in Sweden. We tied 3–3. I played exceptionally well in that game. But Dryden and Espo [Tony Esposito] were the two best goalkeepers at the time and those selections were terrific. I felt no resentment at all about not getting the call.

We had to make some adjustments to how the Russians played. They didn't shoot the puck as hard as we did and they waited for the opportune shot, so a lot of the times, our goalkeepers would move out for the shot and the Russian shooter would hold on to it and move around a little bit. As soon as Dryden and Tony made the adjustments, we got back on track again. We knew we were in for a dogfight.

I think that our pride and determination helped us a lot, especially in that final game. It was such an emotional win. I have never seen grown men cry like our guys did. For about 10 to 15 minutes after the game in our dressing room, it was absolutely emotional. Everybody was in there crying. I've won Stanley Cups and seen some tears of joy, but never like that. We were all overcome, all

Kharlamov was just a terrific player for them and they had Tretiak in the net – he was a super goalkeeper. I don't think anybody figured him out in the early part of the series because we'd never seen his style of goaltending before.

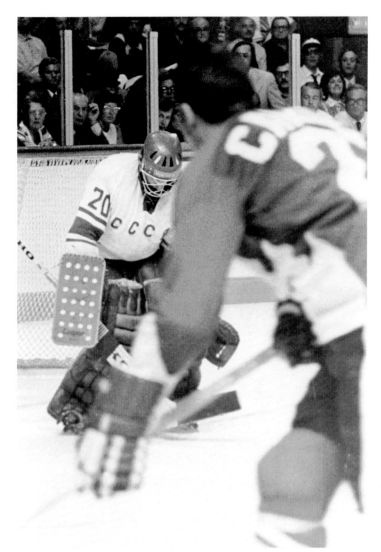

Vladislav Tretiak reacts to a Canadian scoring attempt.

exhausted, all just overjoyed. There was such an emotional feeling in that room after it was over — it was just amazing!

When we came back, we stopped in Toronto and Montreal. There were thousands and thousands of people waiting for us when we came in. The emotion when we got off the plane was just absolutely crazy. It was bedlam in both those cities. It's something that I'll never forget for the rest of my life. Even though I've won Stanley Cups, I don't think that kissing Lord Stanley's old trophy ever had the impact on me that winning with Team Canada did that year.

It took a long time for some of the guys to get back into the swing of the NHL afterward. There was such an emotional letdown that some of the players didn't get pumped again until just a month or so before the playoffs. The emotions had been so high.

One thing I learned in '72 that I took with me as a coach and a general manager was never, never, never underestimate your opponent. That was the number one mistake we made back then. We all learned a lesson from that. No matter what kind of background you have on your opponent, you'd better be able to play your best every single night. If you don't get the effort every night, you're not going to win. You've got to make sure you give 100 percent.

I was very fortunate to play with the Bruins, and won Stanley Cups in '70 and '72. I played until I was 42 years old in the National Hockey League. My last team was Chicago. I coached the Black-hawks in 1979–80 and we went from last place to first place. I've been in Pittsburgh for almost 20 years, outside of 3 and a half years when I went over to Hartford. I've coached 11 years and I've managed 11 years in this league. I'm very blessed that hockey has been very good to me. I've been very fortunate.

GUY LAPOINTE

Guy Lapointe played on six Stanley Cup winners with the Montreal Canadiens during the 1970s. He was a member of the Big Three on defense, along with Larry Robinson and Serge Savard. He was traded to St. Louis in March, 1982 and to Boston in 1983–84. He was inducted into the Hockey Hall of Fame in 1993.

During the 1970s I played on six Stanley Cup winning teams in Montreal. How fortunate can a guy be to reach the NHL and then find himself surrounded by players like Guy Lafleur, Steve Shutt and Jacques Lemaire? To look over your shoulder and see big Ken Dryden guarding the net? And to become known as the one of the Big Three on the Montreal blueline – Serge Savard, Larry Robinson and me, Guy Lapointe. But most of those Stanley Cups came along after Team Canada. In 1972, Guy Lapointe still had lots to learn about hockey.

As if being a young Montreal Canadiens defenseman wasn't enough good fortune for one player to enjoy in the early '70s, how about the added bonus of being selected for Team Canada in 1972? I was just beginning to find my way around the NHL and I was still trying to learn all the tricks of the trade. When I arrived at the Team Canada training camp, I was in awe of all the great names there. Me, I'd just finished my second NHL season and kept wondering, why Guy Lapointe and not some more experienced guy?

I wasn't worrying too much about embarrassing myself against the Russians because we'd all been told they weren't a first-rate team to begin

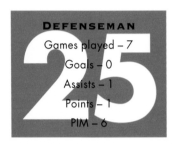

DEFENSEMAN
25
Games played – 7
Goals – 0
Assists – 1
Points – 1
PIM – 6

with, even though Harry Sinden warned us not to get too cocky. I was more worried about looking bad in the scrimmages, trying to stop the best players in the NHL from going around me. I was just hoping to make a good impression.

Well, we all know what happened. How the Soviet players were much stronger, faster and more skillful than we ever imagined. They took us by surprise at the Montreal Forum and really made us look bad. And after their two wins, a loss and a tie in Canada, they became the overconfident team, just like we were before the series started. They actually felt they had us on the ropes – which they did – and that they would win the games in Moscow without much trouble. I guess they didn't realize how determined we were, how hard we'd worked on our conditioning and how much better prepared we were when the second half of the series got underway in Moscow.

Some of our guys hadn't even wanted to play for Team Canada. They had summer hockey schools to run and other commitments and it was a hardship for them to give up a lot of their time in the off season. I heard that Phil and Tony Esposito

They actually felt they had us on the ropes – which they did – and that they would win the games in Moscow without much trouble. I guess they didn't realize how determined we were, how hard we'd worked on our conditioning and how much better prepared we were when the second half of the series got underway in Moscow.

Lapointe racing past Vladimir Vikulov toward the Soviet crease full of determination and expectation.

were reluctant to join the team at first but they are true Canadians and felt they had to show up. Thank God they did. Both were key members of the team and Phil, well, he surpassed anything he'd done before as a player and became one of the most idolized players in the world because of that series.

I played in the first two games and was joined by my friend Serge Savard for game number two in Toronto. Serge was very highly regarded and I

think he helped us put aside the memory of our opening-night disaster in Montreal just by being on the ice. It also helped that another Montreal teammate, Pete Mahovlich, scored one of the most spectacular goals I've ever seen. Killing a penalty, I passed the puck up the boards to Phil Esposito and he tipped it off the boards up to Peter. We were shorthanded and a Soviet goal at that time would have rattled our nerves. But Pete deked around one guy and then barged into Tretiak, slipping the puck into the net. It was an incredible goal that

In Moscow, there were thousands of letters and postcards and telegrams – all wishing us success. And the fans who paid their hard-earned money to come over and cheer us on in person, well, we can never forget them and how much they boosted our spirits. I'm not sure we would have won without them and I'm just thankful we rewarded them in the way they wanted us to, and we were all able to return to Canada with our heads held high.

Lapointe doing a full dive attempt to block a Soviet rush.

sucked the wind right out of the Russians. It's one of my favorite memories of the series. Our confidence got a big boost with the 4–1 victory we earned in game two that night.

We tied the next game in Winnipeg and I got banged around a lot and didn't feel ready to play in game four in Vancouver. That was the game

when the fans really gave it to us and Phil went out and told them what he thought of everything. Not only could I not play, but my friend Serge Savard, in the morning workout, suffered a hairline fracture of his ankle after stopping a puck. Some people said he was through for the series. They didn't know Serge. He came back for game six in Moscow — not fully recovered from his ankle injury but still one of the best defensemen in hockey history. I remember Bobby Clarke calling him "our best defenseman." And that was high praise because Pat Stapleton and Gary Bergman and Bill White were all playing like they'd never played before.

I guess most of the guys will select Paul Henderson's goal in the last minute of the last game as the memory they most cherish. I cherish it too, but the series might have had a much different ending if it hadn't been for the fan support we finally received. In Moscow, there were thousands of letters and postcards and telegrams — all wishing us success. And the fans who paid their hard-earned money to come over and cheer us on in person, well, we can never forget them and how much they boosted our spirits. I'm not sure we would have won without them and I'm just thankful we rewarded them in the way they wanted us to, and we were all able to return to Canada with our heads held high.

Hockey has always been my life. After my 16-year career in the NHL, with Montreal, St. Louis and Boston, I became an assistant coach with the Quebec Nordiques. Then I became head coach and GM of the Longueuil Chevaliers of the Quebec Major Junior League. Our team went to the Memorial Cup tournament in 1986–87. Then I went back to the Nordiques for three seasons. In 1990 I joined the Calgary Flames as a scout and was a member of the coaching staff there for a couple of seasons. Now I'm scouting for the Minnesota Wild of the NHL.

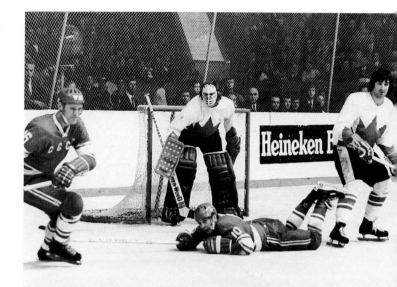

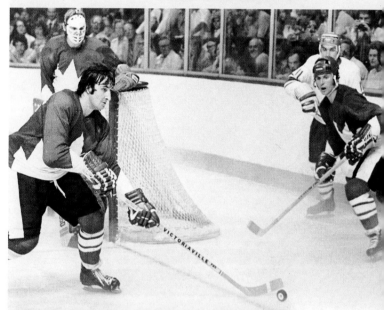

Top and middle: The Soviets keep Ken Dryden and Lapointe busy; bottom: Lapointe, right, with former Summit teammate Richard Martin.

Soviet Union

Game 7: September 26, 1972

Luzhniki Sports Palace, Moscow

After only its second win in the series, Team Canada was on a roll. This time 50,000 telegrams containing good wishes awaited them at their hotel.

On the ice, Team Canada's physical game was starting to take an obvious toll on the Soviets. The Canadians were by now especially adept at disrupting the lightning-quick breakouts from the Soviet end that had plagued them in earlier games. Penalty-killing was outstanding and the Soviets' awesome power play was largely being held in check.

Game seven was rough and tumble and nearly included a brawl. Phil Esposito scored twice in the first period, matching the Soviets' goal output for the frame. The second period was scoreless. Rod Gilbert opened the scoring in the third period but was answered only a few minutes later by a Russian marker.

With the game tied at three apiece and with barely two minutes left to play, Henderson knocked in his second game-winner in as many nights. It was a thing of beauty as he took the puck in all alone, beating two Soviet defenders single-handedly.

Stats

Canada 4, USSR 3
Attendance: 15,000.

FIRST PERIOD
1. Canada, P. Esposito (Ellis, Park) 4:09.
2. USSR, Yakushev (Shadrin) 10:17.
3. USSR, Petrov (Vikulov) 16:27.
4. Canada, P. Esposito (Parise, Savard) 17:34.
Penalties: Mikhailov 2:00; P. Mahovlich and Mishakov 5:16; Mishakov 11:09; P. Esposito 12:39; White 15:45.

SECOND PERIOD
No scoring.
Penalties: Gilbert 00:59; Parise 6:04; Anisin 6:11; P. Esposito and Kuzkin 12:44; Stapleton 15:24.

THIRD PERIOD
5. Canada, Gilbert (Ratelle, Hull) 2:13.
6. USSR, Yakushev (Maltsev, Lutchenko) 5:15.
7. Canada, Henderson 17:54.
Penalties: Bergman 3:26; Gilbert 7:25; Mikhailov and Bergman (majors) 16:26.

SHOTS ON GOAL
Canada: 9-7-9 – 25
USSR: 6-13-12 – 31
Goalies: Canada, T. Esposito; USSR, Tretiak.

Game 8: September 28, 1972

Luzhniki Sports Palace, Moscow

With everything on the line, a curious thing happened. One of the referees simply vanished, and Russian officials replaced him with the referee from game six who seemed to notice only Canadian infractions.

Canada had to win game eight. A tie would mean the Soviets would take the series, as they had scored one more goal than the Canadians. With the referee change, that feat was made even more challenging than if they simply had to face the Soviet juggernaut in a straight game.

J.P. Parise, charged with a minor infraction that gave the Russians a two-man advantage, charged the referee, swinging a stick which he pulled up only just in time to avoid an assault charge. After trading four goals in the first period, Canada fell behind 5–3 in the second.

Scoring one and then two goals in the third period, Canada tied the game with only minutes left. But the Russian goal judge did not turn on the red light to signify the tying goal. A Team Canada official tried to bolt to the time-keeper on the ice to register the goal. He was restrained by gun-toting Russian militia. Pete Mahovlich, on the bench, responded by challenging the militia with his stick. The Canadian official was freed, and the fifth and tying goal was registered.

With less than a minute remaining, Paul Henderson instigated what has become the most famous line change in Canadian hockey history. Calling for Pete Mahovlich to leave the ice, Henderson took his place and immediately joined the attack.

"Here's a shot. Henderson makes a wild stab for it and falls," Foster Hewitt called from his announcer's station. "Here's another shot. Right in front. They score! Henderson scores for Canada!"

Stats

Canada 6, USSR 5
Attendance: 15,000.

FIRST PERIOD
1. USSR, Yakushev (Maltsev, Liapkin) 3:34.
2. Canada, P. Esposito (Park) 6:45.
3. USSR, Lutchenko (Kharlamov) 13:10.
4. Canada, Park (Ratelle, Hull) 16:59.
Penalties: White 2:25; P. Mahovlich 3:01; Petrov 3:44; Parise (minor and game misconduct) 4:10; Tsigankov 6:28; Ellis 9:27; Petrov 9:46; Cournoyer 12:51.

SECOND PERIOD
5. USSR, Shadrin (unassisted) 0:21.
6. Canada, White (Ratelle, Gilbert) 10:32.
7. USSR, Yakushev (unassisted) 11:43.
8. USSR, Vasiliev (unassisted) 16:44.
Penalties: Stapleton 14:58; Kuzkin 18:06.

THIRD PERIOD
9. Canada, P. Esposito (P. Mahovlich) 2:27.
10. Canada, Cournoyer (P. Esposito, Park) 12:56.
11. Canada, Henderson (P. Esposito) 19:26.
Penalties: Mishakov and Gilbert (majors) 3:41; Vasiliev 4:27; Hull and Petrov 15:24.

SHOTS ON GOAL
Canada: 14-8-13 – 35
USSR: 12-10-5 – 27
Goalies: Canada, Dryden; USSR, Tretiak.

FRANK MAHOVLICH

Frank Mahovlich joined the Toronto Maple Leafs in 1957–58 and quickly established himself as one of hockey's greatest scorers. He won the Calder Trophy as top rookie, edging out Bobby Hull for the award. Known as The Big M, he was the most prolific scorer on the Toronto teams that won four Stanley Cups in the 1960s. He was traded to Detroit in March 1968, and was moved again, this time to Montreal, in 1971. Mahovlich was instrumental in the Habs' Cup win that spring. He played on six Cup winners, scored 533 goals and garnered 1,103 points. A Hall of Famer since 1981, today he serves his country as a member of the Canadian Senate.

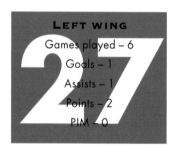

LEFT WING
27
Games played – 6
Goals – 1
Assists – 1
Points – 2
PIM – 0

I believe it was in July when I was called and told they'd like me to be a member of Team Canada in '72. Gosh, everything was up in the air at that time. I had just finished my best NHL season (43 goals and 96 points with the Canadiens) and was getting set to spend some time with my family when this clash with the Russians came up. From that moment on, everything was topsy-turvy that summer. That's how I recall it. Not long after that first phone call, I found myself at a reception in a Toronto hotel room where I met the coaches and organizers and all the other players. That was the beginning and everything just took off from there.

Training camp started right away. I remember it being awfully warm that August. And trying to get all 35 to 40 players on the ice became a real problem. Right off the bat, we didn't know who was going to play very much, and some of the young rookies at the time, future stars like Perreault, Martin, Dionne and Tallon, didn't know whether they were going to get any ice time at all.

I think most of them were just happy to be selected.

Ice time was a real concern among the players and I thought it was a definite morale problem to have so many players on the ice fighting for positions. Everybody was expressing concerns, yet none of the problems appeared to be getting solved. This caused us to have a difficult time as a team getting things in order and getting off the ground.

In training camp, the coaches were dealing with seven or eight forward lines and trying to form the best combinations. Everybody was competing and it was a completely different experience for me. For example, when I went to training camp for the Montreal Canadiens, I knew exactly where I stood with them and I was ready for the season. But at Team Canada's camp, everybody was in limbo. That was a major concern for everybody involved.

In that memorable first game in Montreal, we were very relaxed because we had been informed that we should be able to beat the Russians eight games straight since their goalie was not very

Mahovlich in stride. His size and speed were an imposing combination.

In game two, we were better organized and my brother Pete scored one of the most spectacular goals ever. What was impressive about it was that it was a shorthanded goal. People still talk about it as the second-best goal in the series, next to Henderson's series-winner in Moscow. Pete's big goal kind of picked us up and put us back in the series because if we had lost, going down by two games, I think everybody would have vilified us. But that was a great goal by Pete and a very important win for us.

Vladislav Tretiak has his eyes glued to Mahovlich's stick as Frank goes for the corner.

good. So we were not prepared for that first game. That was a real shocker because we started out so well, scoring two quick goals. Then Harry started to play four or five lines and we just took the Russians for granted. Suddenly, we started to fall apart as a team because, I think, if you don't play your normal game time, you are not going to play up to your highest standard. Gilbert Perreault, for example, was a type of guy who needed 40–45 minutes per game, and he certainly wasn't going to get that with Team Canada. He likes to carry the play, and if he doesn't touch the puck, then it's not his game. His performance is thrown way off.

In game two, we were better organized and my brother Pete scored one of the most spectacular goals ever. What was impressive about it was that it was a shorthanded goal. People still talk about it as the second-best goal in the series, next to Henderson's series-winner in Moscow. Pete's big goal kind of picked us up and put us back in the series because if we had lost, going down by two games, I think everybody would have vilified us. But that was a great goal by Pete and a very important win for us.

In Winnipeg they got the jump on us again by going out there and practicing on the Winnipeg ice. We stayed back in Toronto overnight and practiced on the Toronto ice prior to leaving for Winnipeg. It would have been much better for us to fly to Winnipeg, get a feel for the ice there and the city and then play the game. But we were able to come out of that game with a tie.

I remember a truly outstanding goal that a winger named Kharlamov scored in Winnipeg. I'll never forget the play that led up to it. Phil Esposito and I had the Russians pinned in their end and we both went after this Russian defenseman. Just as we piled into him, he fired the puck across the ice to the far boards near the blueline. There was no player there but the puck bounced up to the red-line in the center zone and was caught on the fly by Kharlamov, who was motoring at full speed. It had to be a planned play. The Russians must have practiced that damn play because Phil and I clobbered this defenseman and when we turned around a split second later the puck was in our net and Kharlamov was celebrating it. It happened so fast nobody could believe it. That was just a phenomenal goal.

Sometimes in hockey the media and the fans can jump all over you, rightly or wrongly, like they did following our loss in Vancouver. That was in game four. They booed us off the ice there, and of course Phil Esposito had to come out and make his big

The Little M and The Big M, brothers on and off the ice, relax before a game.

speech, trying to explain how we all felt and how frustrated we were.

In Vancouver, I developed a bad allergy that forced me to seek medical treatment. So I stayed back in Canada for a couple of days before rejoining the team in Sweden. For some reason, this allergy hit me hard and both of my eyes were swollen shut. At the time I didn't know what was the matter with me. It wasn't until I had some tests done 2 or 3 years later that I found out from a doctor that the enemy was ragweed. It was amazing how it just drained all my energy. I've grown immune to it over the last 20 years but it hit me pretty hard just before we went to Sweden. My eyes were closed and bloodshot and were constantly itchy. It was a pretty severe attack, so I stayed back and missed a couple of days in Sweden.

The two Swedish games were really brutal. I remember the big incident when Cashman got cut because a player had speared him in the tongue. Vic Hadfield attacked Sjoberg and that was another terrible incident. The papers carried large spreads about these attacks and started to pick on us about them. It was self-destructive, and we weren't on the right track yet.

The Canadian ambassador in Sweden, Mr. Ford, tried to defend us but he had to be diplomatic. In Russia, Mrs. Ford, the ambassador's wife, was a tough little gal, and she knew how to handle those Russians. She would tell them, "Get out of the way!" and "Let this person in!" and "Go stand over there!" If we had hired her as our manager we would not have had a problem, believe me.

I was happy to see Peter play such consistently good hockey. He played in all eight games, and he was just outstanding. If you go right to the last game and see the shot that he took from a Russian defenseman, before he gave the puck to Esposito at the 2:27 mark of the third period, if you watch that replay, it was typical of Peter. He set a lot of guys up and then Esposito scored that goal, which was very important because it led us to our big comeback.

Throughout the series, we would have discussions to try to analyze the Russians and their play, and what they were trying to do to us psychologically.

Pete played very well because he never let anything bother him. He just continued to play his strong game like the ones he played in Montreal and Toronto. He and Cournoyer, and Henderson and Ellis – they were all outstanding.

Pete is a laid-back, happy-go-lucky type guy and I take things much more seriously, but I didn't let the Russians get under my skin. I spent my time trying to figure them out. I know people said, "Well, Frank's really bothered," but I was only bothered in trying to get the team fully prepared. We were simply too relaxed at first. I was concerned in Montreal when I came out to the meeting and nobody showed up on time. And this was a team meeting. I was not used to that. I was brought up under Punch Imlach and Toe Blake and they were adamant that you had to be prepared.

Also in Montreal, when I tried to get on the ice for a practice session, the Russians would not get off the ice. It was our turn to get on the ice, even though there were only three or four of us ready to go when the whole team was supposed to be there.

There were a lot of little things to indicate we were just not prepared. We were not acting like the professional teams I knew. The Russians were really prepared, everything for them ran like clockwork. They were on the bus and on the ice on time and in place, whereas we were not that disciplined. We were all so relaxed. We were simply not ready for them.

We had our wives meet us in Russia. I got off the plane in Moscow and my wife Marie was already there. Somebody had complained because they were going to put all the wives in one hotel and the team in another but they finally got everything straightened out.

I remember a truly outstanding goal scored in Winnipeg. The Russians must have practiced that damn play because Phil and I clobbered this defenseman and when we turned around a split second later the puck was in our net and Kharlamov was celebrating it. It happened so fast nobody could believe it.

Mahovlich gets around Vladimir Lutchenko, putting more pressure on a preoccupied Vladislav Tretiak.

Another thing I recall was the food problem. We had a very difficult time getting the food we'd brought along. I was there again in '74 with the WHA and food was always a problem. Getting the steaks we'd brought along was a major undertaking. When we got them, they had been sliced in half lengthwise and when we complained, they simply cut them in half the other way. Finally, by the last game, we got our whole steaks. They wouldn't let us have our beer when we wanted it, either, and when they finally got it to us, much of it had gone missing.

Everybody had complaints about the refereeing. John Ferguson, our assistant coach and a very competitive fellow, was incensed over some of the calls. The officials were absolutely brutal. Some of the calls astonished us. They would never be seen in the NHL, so John and the rest of us had good reason to be upset. But John was especially livid.

In the thick of the final game battle, I was on the bench sitting beside my brother. Peter was doing up his laces or something so he wasn't aware of the commotion in the stands, until I said, "Peter, look!

Nailing the coffin shut: Guy Lapointe, Stan Mikita, Yvan Cournoyer and Serge Savard celebrate Mahovlich's goal giving the Canadians a 4–1 lead in game two.

They've got the Eagle!" I saw these two soldiers dragging Eagleson from the stands. There were a few people standing up and there was a bit of a ruckus going on, and I wondered what in the hell they were doing. They had picked up Eagleson by his arms and he was kicking and scratching and I was telling this to Peter. He asked, "Where?" and I said, "Right over there by the penalty box." Without thinking, Pete just jumped up, ran over to the penalty box, jumped over the glass and got right in front of the soldiers. He raised his stick and hollered, "Let him go!" And they did. When Eagleson was freed, he jumped right over the bench, slid across the ice and sat down beside me. I said, "Al, you're okay now. Just sit here and be quiet." He was white as a sheet and speechless. Pete was just reacting to the situation. It was

amazing. That's what happened. All people saw on TV was the one-finger salute Eagleson gave. Peter didn't see what started it — Eagleson reacting to the delayed red light following our goal. He just took off to save him.

Despite all our difficulties over there, I love Russia, I hope they solve all their problems. They are very hardworking people. I went back in '99 for a reunion. We had a great time and they treated us superbly, compared to '72 and '74. So if they can get things turned around, I'm sure it will be a great country once again.

The Russians really impressed me in that '72 series with their system. And even back in '57 when I had a chance to watch them, I thought they were doing the right things on the ice and they were on their way. The way they studied the game and the way they applied themselves was impressive. I think they were innovators of hockey. If I were a coach I would use a lot of their ideas – like the cross-ice pass off the boards and up into the center zone, which was a set play. Without even looking they could gamble on that move and it caught us off guard.

I loved Russia and got a great sense of the country. We went to museums and visited the city. I think they are a very cultured people. Even in '99 at the reunion, we went back to the Bolshoi [Theater]. The Russians have a wonderful sense of humor. What happens on stage often happens in real life.

I can recall going to the circus and Al Eagleson was at one end and Harold Ballard was sitting at the other. Three clowns came out. One had a whistle like a referee and the other one was picking up balls. The one who had the whistle was telling the other two clowns what to do. Well, he dropped his whistle and another clown picked it up. So he became the boss. And as this funny act was going on, Eagleson and Ballard, from opposite ends of the performing area, were yelling at each other about who was the boss. That was hilarious.

After the series in '72 I had 2 more good years with the Canadiens and 4 more in the WHA with the Toronto Toros and the Birmingham Bulls. Then I ran my travel agency in Toronto for over 20 years. I retired from my business and was appointed to the Senate in '98. I was in New York at the Waldorf, at a big annual Canadian Society Dinner at which they honor a top hockey personality every year. A phone call from Ottawa brought news about the Senate appointment. I was told not to say anything – it was a secret. When I got to the

dinner, Neil Smith, then the manager of the New York Rangers, walked up to me and said, "My mother just called from Toronto. She said she heard over the radio that you've been named to the Senate. Congratulations." I was amazed. I thought my wife and I were the only people who knew.

Peter and Frank Mahovlich together at a golf banquet north of Toronto.

So far, it's been a role I've truly enjoyed and one I take very seriously. I just got back from being in Edmonton for three days and listening to the caucus on what the game plan is for the coming year and it really is exciting. Any sport is so much like politics. Quite often, Lester Pearson used to watch baseball and the moves the manager used to make with his team, and it's the same with Chrétien. I think he was a hockey player in his younger days and it helps him because he can use what he learned from playing hockey as a team game in the game of politics.

PETER MAHOVLICH

Peter Mahovlich reached NHL stardom after being traded from Detroit to Montreal in 1969. He helped the Canadiens win the Stanley Cup four times in a row in the 1970s, performing on a line with Guy Lafleur and Jacques Lemaire. Those clubs are considered to be among the league's all-time best teams. He was traded to Pittsburgh (for Pierre Larouche) in November 1977 and finished his career back in Detroit. In 884 games, Mahovlich scored 288 goals and added 485 assists for 773 points.

CENTER
20
Games played – 7
Goals – 1
Assists – 1
Points – 2
PIM – 4

I believe the biggest highlight of my hockey career was in 1972 when we were able to win a series that became so important in hockey. No one expected the series to be as exciting and as memorable as it turned out to be. The first day of September, everybody thought we were going to win easily, but on September 3 we realized we were going to have to go through a battle — a huge battle, and one that everyone was talking about.

In the Montreal Forum for the opening game, for the first 5 minutes we were on top of the roof, and the next 25 minutes we were underneath the ice. The loss that night was a shocker. For me, it was also a very discouraging time in Vancouver, during another loss. That was the one game I didn't play in and being in the stands listening to the people boo us — really boo us — and hearing some of their snide comments about the players that were on the ice, I felt really bad and discouraged. I guess we all did.

But we all got a huge lift when Phil was interviewed after that game and told the Canadian public exactly how he felt. Phil always speaks straight from the heart and he was right on the mark that night. He spoke for all of us.

People often ask me about the goal I scored in game two. Most have forgotten that it was a short-handed goal. What got it going was that we had just given up a power play goal about a minute earlier, and suddenly we were hit with another penalty. So it was a critical situation. Phil and I

Peter Mahovlich at the Hockey Hall of Fame, Toronto.

Mahovlich breaks through the Russian defense, Moscow.

Coming off the very lowest moments, the bitterness and humiliation we suffered in Montreal in game one where we lost big-time, that spectacular goal by Pete helped us to a victory at Maple Leaf Gardens. It was a goal I'll never forget, an uplifting moment for the team in a game we urgently needed to win. – *Harry Sinden*

Aleksandr Yakushev cannot stop a Mahovlich shot with Yvan Cournoyer racing in full support.

talked about trying to hang on to the puck and not throwing it away to give them possession. I was not thinking at all about scoring when Phil threw the puck around the boards. I grabbed it and looked up and saw a one-on-one situation with their defenseman. I thought I would fake a shot and see what he would do. He flinched and I was able to get around him, but not by much. I didn't have time to think; I was going in on the right side of Tretiak. I made him move back to his left and when I moved right, I piled right into him and

slipped the puck in behind him. The defenseman I went around got injured and never played in another game. One Russian reporter said it was a national tragedy — for the defense guy.

Who was the most impressive player? Well, for me it was Phil Esposito. He was huge in that series, an inspiring leader on and off ice. He really was phenomenal.

For the Soviets, Kharlamov was a great forward. Tretiak was a major surprise. We had all heard

Mahovlich in an all-out skirmish as Aleksandr Yakushev and Jean-Paul Parise anticipate receiving the puck.

that he was not supposed to be a very talented goaltender but he was terrific — very solid in every game.

I often wonder how the series might have been played if John Ferguson had decided to be a playing-coach for Team Canada. I suppose there might have been a little more blood spilled, and I doubt it would have been ours.

When I think of the impact playing for Team Canada has had on my life, I think of what a great opportunity it was to represent my country. Back then, you'll recall, we weren't allowed to play in the Olympics, and that '72 series started it all. Playing for your country is the ultimate for any

athlete. That was a great honor for me, and the fact that the Canadian people voted us the team of the century was a wonderful tribute. Overall, after a slow start, it turned out to be a great experience. It helped us immensely that there were about 3,000 Canadians in the stands at Moscow cheering wildly. That support was really incredible.

I've spent most of my life in hockey. For the past eight years I've been scouting for various teams — the Edmonton Oilers, the Tampa Bay Lightning, and the Atlanta Thrashers — which I really enjoy. The Thrashers have been very good to me.

RICHARD MARTIN

Richard (Rick) Martin, a Buffalo Sabre, set a rookie goal-scoring record with 44 in 1971–72. Martin was the top scorer on the Sabres' famed French Connection line (with Gilbert Perreault and Rene Robert) in the 1970s. Injuries forced him out of the game after a brief stint with the L.A. Kings. In 685 games, he scored 384 goals and garnered 701 points.

After I retired from the NHL, it took me some time to find something I really wanted to do, and finally I got into the computer consulting business. I've been involved in that for the past 11 years. Our company has headquarters in Buffalo, but we have offices in Albany and Cleveland, too. When I began I didn't know anything about computers but my boss, a good friend of mine, said, "Don't worry about it. You'll learn." And I did.

A serious knee injury forced me to retire from the NHL in 1982 after 10 years with the Buffalo Sabres and a handful of games with the Los Angeles

LEFT WING

Games played – 0

36

Kings. Of course, I'd liked to have played a few more seasons and perhaps topped 500 goals [Rick scored 384 goals in 685 games] but it wasn't meant to be. Fortunately, most of my career was spent on the French Connection line with the Sabres. You couldn't find better linemates anywhere than Rene Robert and Gilbert Perreault.

I was only 20 when I was asked to join Team Canada in 1972 and I was honored to be selected but disappointed not to play in any of the games. It was a tough situation for me, because I reported in tremendous shape and was really anxious to play. But it turned out to be such a tight series, to everyone's surprise, that Harry felt he had to go with his veteran players.

It was a great experience for me, being on the ice with the best players in the NHL, then flying to Sweden and Moscow. I was one of the players who left early because Buffalo GM Punch Imlach pressured me to come home. When I learned that I wouldn't be getting into any games, and Punch heard about it, he called to say, "Get your ass back to Buffalo and into training camp." So I asked Harry and the

Richard Martin at the Hockey Hall of Fame, 2000.

When I saw the Russians play for the first time, I said, "My God, they are in phenomenal shape." And their execution was tremendous. It was like watching robots play at full speed, passing well and shooting accurately. They were like a well-oiled machine.

Relentless in front of the Canadian net, Vladimir Shadrin tussles with Brad Park as Aleksandr Yakushev scouts for a loose puck.

others, "Do you mind if I go back?" and they said, "Sure. No problem. Thanks for coming. Good luck this season." That sort of thing. Nobody made a big deal of it. Still, it was a tough decision. If I'd been an older player, been around for a few years, I would have stayed. And maybe have played.

I didn't realize the magnitude of my decision until I arrived back in Canada. I flew into Halifax where I planned to stay overnight to visit my sister in Truro. When I got off the plane I found 50 microphones and 18 cameras thrust in my face. That was a shock.

As for watching the Russian players, I was impressed with all of them. Their conditioning was very impressive. As good as my own – and I

was in great shape when I reported to the Team Canada training camp. When I saw them play for the first time, I said, "My God, they are in phenomenal shape." And their execution was tremendous. It was like watching robots play at full speed, passing well and shooting accurately. They were like a well-oiled machine. If some of our guys were a little complacent in training camp, they soon caught up and had enough skill and sheer determination to win the series.

I'd love to have been more involved – every hockey players wants his ice time – and that's my only regret. But I have no regrets about any of the time I spent traveling with and learning from the outstanding players on that club.

HOWIE MEEKER

Howie Meeker scored 27 goals in his rookie season as a Leaf (1946–47) and won the Calder Trophy that season. On January 18, 1947, he set a rookie record with five goals in a game. After eight years as a player, he was asked to coach the Leafs in 1956–57 and became the club's general manager the next season. Following his NHL career, he became a member of Parliament and, later, a television broadcaster. For many years he was an outspoken commentator on *Hockey Night in Canada* and other broadcasting outlets.

COMMENTATOR

Well, I just couldn't believe my eyes after the first period of the first game. I saw them (the Russian team) practice once and I knew we could be in trouble. But in that first game they came out of their own zone as good as or better than we did. They took our defensemen wide and went around them like a hoop around a barrel. Team Canada scored on their first two chances and both goals were… aaah… questionable kinds of goals. After that it was no contest. I was shocked just like all of Canada was shocked.

In Vancouver they were practically booed off the ice and deservedly so. Then Phil Esposito took over. He told Canada, "Hey, we were caught with our pants down. And we're in half shape but we're going to get in top shape. And, believe me, we're going to win this cotton-pickin' thing." And they did. As far as I'm concerned, Esposito turned in the greatest effort by an individual in any sport. Without Espo we don't win that series. He was absolutely the best performer I've ever seen in any series.

We had a lot of guys play the best hockey they ever played in that series. The little red-headed guy from Chicago – Pat Stapleton – that little son-of-a-gun played super hockey. As did Serge Savard, the big Canadiens' star. He was the key man back on defense, coming back from a leg injury he suffered in Vancouver. A lot of people don't know he had to play hurt in the games in Moscow.

What hurt the Russians badly was losing their best player, Kharlamov. It was a very tough, mean, good player for Team Canada, Bobby Clarke, who took out Kharlamov with a chop to the ankle. Kharlamov was their best goal scorer, their best player to go wide around a not-too-mobile Canadian defense and that was a big blow to the Russians. It's funny, you don't see Clarke's check on Kharlamov in replays of the game. I think the people who edited the plays said, "Look boys, let's burn that one."

The goaltending was *comme ci, comme ça*. Dryden was good at times, and then not so good. But I'll say this. The key was Canada being down two goals with a period to play in game eight. And Dryden came up with three great saves after Canada got within one goal. If he doesn't make those stops, we don't win the series.

The impact of the series on hockey? Nothing at all. We didn't learn anything from it. We still haven't learned anything from it. If you want offense, you go to Europe. If you want defense, with tough, hard-working guys, you go to Canada. So I guess there was one impact. The NHL owners figured, if we're going to expand, we have to go to Europe to find some talent.

The game turned into a war that the Canadians paid for in unprecedented penalties. Bobby Clarke received a minor and a misconduct penalty after an altercation with Valeri Kharlamov in game six.

The impact of the series on hockey? Nothing at all. We didn't learn anything from it. We still haven't learned anything from it. If you want offense, you go to Europe. If you want defense, with tough, hard-working guys, you go to Canada. So I guess there was one impact. The NHL owners figured, if we're going to expand, we have to go to Europe to find some talent.

You've got to give Team Canada full marks for what they achieved. Everybody in the world counted them out except the players themselves.

They showed people it's our game and we play it better than anybody else. But gee, the ability to be able to say that grows less and less until we start teaching our kids the skills of the game. Until we start doing that, we're going to be in big trouble in international hockey.

STAN MIKITA

Stan Mikita was born in Czechoslovakia, moving to Canada in 1948 to live with relatives. He soon became a great player in junior hockey and went on to an illustrious 22-year career with the Chicago Blackhawks. In 1960–61 he helped the Hawks win their first Stanley Cup in 23 years. In 1966–67 he became the first NHL player to win three major trophies in one season: the Hart, the Ross and the Lady Byng. He repeated the feat the following season. He played in 1,394 games, scored 541 goals and added 926 assists for 1,467 points. Mikita was elected to the Hockey Hall of Fame in 1983.

After I retired from the NHL in 1979–80, after 22 years with the Chicago Blackhawks, I went into the golf business. For years I was a pro manager of the Kemper Lakes Golf Course which is in the suburbs of Chicago. The 1989 PGA Championships were held there. It's an excellent golf course. Shortly afterward I decided

RIGHT WING

21

Games played – 2
Goals – 0
Assists – 1
Points – 1
PIM – 0

to leave the golf business in 1987. I became a manufacturers rep with a private business named Stan Mikita Enterprises. I am still running that business and I have my two younger children, Jane and Christopher, helping me out. My son Scott Mikita is married to Sarah Pfisterer, and they are both actors appearing in roles on Broadway. Sarah starred in *Show Boat* and *Phantom of the Opera*. Scott is with *Phantom* full time. They have a little girl who is now five months old.

When I look back on the highs and lows of the Team Canada experience, I think the low for me was when the man who was supposed to be our leader was picked up by the Russian KGB at rinkside in Moscow — and they let him go! They should have kept him somewhere and thrown the key away. Bradley Park would agree with me on that.

The best part of the series was the anticipation of playing in my first game, which was game two in Toronto. I was thinking back to my heritage – I'm a Slovak – and what the USSR stood for at that time

Stan Mikita accepting his trophy at the Team of the Century induction ceremonies, 2000.

with the Communist regime. Russia invaded my homeland in 1968. Jaramir Jagr wears number 68 for that reason. The prelude to that game was most important to me, but once we stepped on the ice it was just a game. It wasn't life or death.

After we won in Moscow, I had a chance to go back to Prague with Team Canada and we played an exhibition game there. I was proud of that. And Harry Sinden named me captain of the team for that game, so my whole family came to Prague to see me. My mother was still alive then. She and my sister and my brother and their families got a chance to see the game and visit with us for a few hours. It was a very emotional day for me.

After the series I was living in Chicago. The series didn't have much effect on the fans living there. Only the rock-solid fan really cared about the outcome. But all of Canada came to an absolute standstill at the end of the game after Henderson's goal. And that was a very proud moment for me, just to be associated with that event. Especially to see how the Canadian people got together. It was a bonding of the country.

My friend Brian Glennie likes to tell a story at hockey banquets about something that happened to us in Sweden. We were working out one day and I tried a new move on Brian that caught him off guard. I was really sick with the flu and when I moved in on him I ended up throwing up on his skates. Then in a regular season game later that year, I moved in on him and when he jumped in front of me, I joked, "Watch out, big guy, I have that Swedish move down pat now so you better step back." That got him thinking.

Phil Esposito did spectacular things out on the ice during that series. He would hold up big tough

Mikita taking a breather during a Team Canada practice.

guys and just stand up to them instead of looking for that open spot like he usually did. He really played well defensively, and his offense was just excellent. He impressed me and became a great leader during that series. He was quite vocal. Whenever we were all together he was the first guy to speak up and say what he had to say. Before that, Phil was kind of laid-back, a guy who would show you with his talent rather than with his voice.

When Stan Mikita played in Czechoslovakia in our final exhibition game, I had tears in my eyes. Stan received a 10-minute standing ovation and it was very emotional. And here's how Harry picked the players for that game. We were all hungover so he lined us up and looked us over. "You look all right to play," he'd say to one of us, and, "You'd better sit out," he'd say to another. That's how he got his roster. I must have looked pretty sober so I got to play. – *Dennis Hull*

Mikita's first of two games was in Toronto. Here, his teammates Bill White, Rod Seiling, Tony Esposito, Gary Bergman and Pat Stapleton celebrate that Canadian win.

As for the guys who quit on us, I think it was said at a meeting, "If you guys want to go home, go ahead. That's no problem." I do think Harry wanted to keep them there for the sake of team unity. But I don't think their leaving had any effect on the rest of the players. I did not hear one guy say, "Look at those bastards. They're bailing out on us." Remember, they were under pressure from their NHL bosses to get back as soon as possible, especially if they weren't getting into our games. The team didn't shun anyone after he quit and went home, players like Hadfield, Perreault, Martin and Guevremont.

JEAN-PAUL PARISE

Jean-Paul Parise spent several seasons in the minors before joining Boston for 3 games in 1965–66. Claimed by Oakland in June 1967, he was immediately traded to Toronto, where he played in 1 game. He became a regular with the Minnesota North Stars in 1968–69, playing with the Stars for the next eight years. He spent the following four seasons with the New York Islanders and finished his career with one season in Cleveland and a final season in Minnesota. He played in 890 games and scored 238 goals.

My best memory would be that I played in the eighth game. I didn't finish the game but I played in it. Originally, when Harry Sinden had called me and invited me to play, I thought I'd be lucky to play in one game and it probably would be in Sweden, or perhaps in the wind-up game in Czechoslovakia. For me to have played in six of the eight games was just such a tremendous feeling of accomplishment. The fact that I played with Yvan Cournoyer and Phil Esposito, my gosh, it doesn't get much better than that for a journeyman player, does it? I was a pretty good player but not a world-class player, and to play the last four

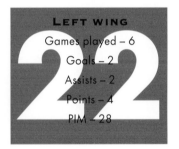

LEFT WING
22
Games played – 6
Goals – 2
Assists – 2
Points – 4
PIM – 28

games in Moscow and to play with those two guys was tremendous for me.

I don't think that anybody knew what the impact of the final game was going to be — what it all had come down to. For me, the fact that I was tossed from the game by the referee — a terrible ref named Kompalla — was a total negative. He gave me a penalty and I broke my stick on the ice and then faked a swing at him. I never planned to hit him. I just wanted to show him we'd had enough. It was bullshit that he was the ref, and if they weren't going to play fair, we weren't either. But then, because of the fact that we came back from being two goals behind and then went on to win the series, the disappointment of my penalty was very short-lived. I appreciated those good players and how they made me feel that losing my temper didn't matter. The total focus of the team was that we were going to beat the Russians and become victorious. I didn't appreciate getting kicked out of the game, obviously I was very distressed, but then to go back and have this tremendous feeling of victory an hour later was just outstanding.

Parise was tossed from game eight after threatening the referee with his stick: "I just wanted to show him we'd had enough!"

Parise manipulates the puck while Paul Henderson and Anatoli Firsov rally for positions.

So all the debates and disputes over the referees and the kind of experience that all Canadian teams in international hockey have always had – Canada gets more penalties; we play a different kind of game; the rules are different – something that was simmering boiled over and exploded. J.P. Parise, always a nose-to-the-grindstone kind of player, suddenly becomes the center of things, swinging his stick at the referee, stopping just before contact is made. *– Ken Dryden*

Parise in position as the play develops around Vladimir Lutchenko, Vladislav Tretiak and Phil Esposito.

The key person on our team was Phil Esposito in terms of leadership. And then Bobby Clarke's line did a lot of damage, too. I don't think most people realized how good Bobby Clarke, Ron Ellis and Paul Henderson were. And Paul scoring all those goals. I mean, that was impressive. You would never predict that would happen. To me, as far as the Canadian team was concerned, these were the four guys who were the most impressive.

For the Russians, Kharlamov was just out of this world. He was a tremendous player. But the most complete player was Aleksandr Yakushev. He was a very, very big player for those days, and he was outstanding. As well, the play of Tretiak really surprised us. He was impressive. But Tretiak allowed a lot of goals, too. Going into the final two minutes of the final game, we were told by some Russian that if we tied the game, the Russians would claim a win because they had scored one more goal in the whole series than we had. Someone told him to shove off. It made Henderson's last-minute goal all that much more important. Tretiak did play very well, but so did our goalies. Tony Esposito and Ken Dryden were every bit as outstanding, if not even better.

Jean-Paul Parise.

I was nicknamed "J.P." by Harry Sinden. I played for a number of years for Harry in the minors, and I think he is a wonderful hockey person. Harry Sinden and Wren Blair gave me a chance to play pro. I was never a prolific goal-scorer, but Harry gave me a chance to play for Team Canada and I'll forever be thankful.

To this day, I'm recognized. I was just a journeyman. I averaged 50 points a season during my career — basically, 20 goals a year. I lasted a long time — almost 13 years. But you know, guys who score 50 points a season and 20 goals a year just disappear in terms of memory from the fans. The fact that I did play in the '72 series gave me a much higher profile in hockey than I would have had otherwise. Having played with those wonderful players made me work harder and, in my mind, if I worked harder, I would compete at a higher level than I had competed in previous years. Maybe it worked. I hope so.

After I retired as a player, I remained with the Minnesota North Stars as an assistant coach. Then we all got dismissed in 1987–88. I was assistant coach with Herb Brooks during that year. By then, I had two young children who were four and two at the time. I had to decide whether I was going to stay in hockey, perhaps in coaching. Then I got out. I felt I should be helping to raise my two children. I sold commercial insurance for eight years. Currently, I am director of the hockey program in a private school, called Shattuck-St. Mary's in Faribault, Minnesota. It has a total enrollment of 300 and we have eight teams and about 165 hockey players here. We have six boys' teams and two girls' teams. In two of the last three years, we have won the midget nationals. And in the last two years, we have won the Max tournament in Calgary for midget AAA. We have the best hockey program in the United States. We've hired professional coaches — former NHL veteran Murray Eaves works for us. It's been wonderful for me.

Both my sons are doing very well in hockey. Jordan is a good goalie. He's going to be playing Junior A this year in Surrey, British Columbia. And Zack is going into his senior year. He's been heavily recruited by colleges in the United States. He's probably the number one recruited kid in the country. Right now, he can go to any college he wants to. He's a good player and he's represented our country in Germany. I'm very lucky.

BRAD PARK

Brad Park was one of the top NHL defensemen of his era and was a league all-star in seven of eight seasons in the 1970s. On November 7, 1975, Park was involved in a multiplayer deal that saw him don a Boston Bruins' jersey. In 1983 he joined the Detroit Red Wings as a free agent and later coached the Wings briefly. He was inducted into the Hockey Hall of Fame in 1988. He played in 1,113 games in 17 seasons, scoring 213 goals and 896 points.

The best moment of the series, the one that I really enjoy remembering, is when Henderson scored the winning goal in the last game. The relief of that was unbelievable. We were losing 5–3 and everybody had mixed emotions about winning. Our aim was to tie up the game, but that was short-lived. Between periods the Russians came down and stated that if the game was tied, they would still end up winning the series because they had more goals. Normally we might play it for the tie, but now we had to play all-out and attack, which is how we ended up winning the series. We just kept pressing them and hounding them, and that's what led to the Henderson goal.

My biggest shock came after the first game. I was a spectator and I soon realized it was not going to be a cakewalk. This was going to be serious hockey. At the end of the first period I went down to the dressing room with Gary Bergman — he was my defense partner and later an outstanding player in the series — and he said to me, "So what do you think?" I said, "We're in big, big trouble, Gary. They're coming at us in waves, they're just flying at us. Bergy, we're going to have to come up

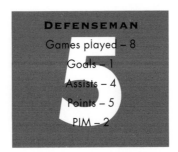

DEFENSEMAN
Games played – 8
Goals – 1
Assists – 4
Points – 5
PIM – 2

with some super efforts to get out of this."

In Moscow I remember the distractions, like the intercoms that would come on in the middle of the night, disturbing our sleep. Then the phone would ring and there'd be nobody on the line. These things drove Phil Esposito crazy. He hated it over there. I think the fact that we had too many players also created a problem. Everybody wanted to play. Why wouldn't they? I mean, you can't take a

Aleksandr Maltsev loses his stick between Park's legs as Valeri Kharlamov tries to sneak past Jean Ratelle.

A stickless Park prevents Aleksandr Yakushev from making any sudden moves.

At the end of the first period I went down to the dressing room with Gary Bergman and he said to me, "So what do you think?" I said, "We're in big, big trouble, Gary. They're coming at us in waves, they're just flying at us. Bergy, we're going to have to come up with some super efforts to get out of this."

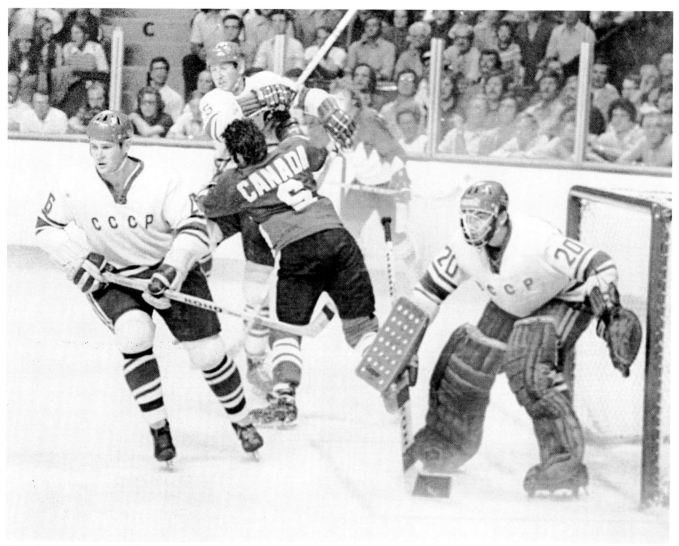

Park demonstrates his offensive abilities, causing havoc around the Soviet goal crease.

bunch of old war-horses and make them into a bunch of cheerleaders.

The series, surprisingly, changed my feelings toward my NHL rivals at the time. Afterward, guys who I disliked, or just didn't care if they were better players than I was, ended up being some of my closest friends. I formed a lot of life-long bonds

with them and I respected their talents. Even the Soviets, who did what they had to do in the heat of the moment, kicking and throwing punches — I gained a lot of respect for them as competitors and skilled players. Tretiak was unbelievable as a young 20-year-old goalie in that series. He was just spectacular.

Park takes control of the puck and steers the play toward center ice with Peter Mahovlich by his side.

Brad Park (right).

I was 24 years old after Team Canada in '72. I brought back with me an abundance of knowledge, some things I hadn't thought much about before. I really started to concentrate on power plays and being able to one-time the puck from different locations. Being with the Rangers was special because we were a puck-control team much like the Soviets. I spent some time afterward in Boston with Don Cherry, which was really interesting. I played eight years with the Bruins.

Then, late in my career, I went to Detroit for a couple of seasons as an aging veteran and helped the Red Wings make the playoffs in Detroit. It's hard to believe the Wings had missed the playoffs 15 times in the previous 17 seasons — a woeful record. I tried coaching the Wings after I retired but lasted only half a season. The politics there caused a lot of interference.

Now I spend more time with my family. After coaching I moved back to Boston. My wife and I had five kids and one of them was disabled so I didn't want to be traveling around in the coaching position. It just didn't make sense. I wanted some stability for my family. And I think that was the best decision I made, to get out of hockey and allow my kids to grow up and enjoy their lives.

GILBERT PERREAULT

Gilbert Perreault was the first player selected by the Buffalo Sabres (in the Entry Draft) when they joined the NHL in 1970. He went on to become the Buffalo career-leader in almost every category – games (1,191), goals (512), assists (814) and points (1,326). With Rene Robert and Rick Martin as his wings, he centered the potent French Connection line during the 1970s. He was inducted into the Hockey Hall of Fame in 1990.

I think the Team Canada '72 series was a learning experience for all of us. I was a very young player at the time, just a kid, and to play with all these great players was a big thrill for me. It was a great experience. However, I felt that they had too many players in training camp, 35 in all. I only got into two games so I guess my biggest disappointment was the fact that I did not get to play more. But I knew in my heart that my turn would come, meaning a couple of years later.

My biggest moment in the series came in the Vancouver game. Harry gave me some ice time when we got behind 2–0 – he thought I could skate with the Russians – and I capped off an end-to-end rush with a goal against Tretiak. I circled the net and my centering pass caromed off one of their defensemen. It was the highlight of the series for me.

I singled out Phil Esposito as one of the great leaders on the team. Yvan Cournoyer was also great. As for the Russians, I really admired the left winger Yakushev – he had great moves and could really fly down the wing. Unlike some who thought Tretiak would be a sieve in goal, I had played against him as a junior and I knew how

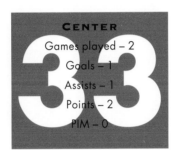

CENTER
33
Games played – 2
Goals – 1
Assists – 1
Points – 2
PIM – 0

good he could be, so I was not surprised that he was one of the top players in the series.

As for leaving Moscow before the series was over, it was a tough decision to make. At one point, I was one of 10 or 12 guys who decided we'd come home. We knew we weren't going to get any more ice time, so why stay? But in the end, only 4 of us came back. I was happy to hear J.P. Parise defend me. He said, "I roomed with Gilbert Perreault and I know him. And he's no quitter."

Peter Mahovlich and Perreault stir up things below the Soviet blueline.

I singled out Phil Esposito as one of the great leaders on the team. Yvan Cournoyer was also great. As for the Russians, I really admired the left winger Yakushev – he had great moves and could really fly down the wing.

Evgeni Zimin tries to clear Yvan Cournoyer from blocking Vladislav Tretiak as Perreault plans his next move.

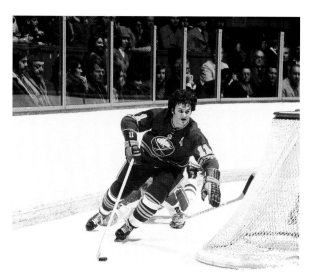

Perreault seen here in his Buffalo Sabers uniform retired with an impressive hockey career, scoring more than 500 goals.

Perhaps I had been selected to Team Canada because I had won the Calder Trophy as Rookie of the Year in '71. After the series I played in the NHL, retiring in '86. I am quite proud of my NHL career. I played in over 1,000 games and scored 512 goals. My only regret is that I never played on a Stanley Cup-winning team.

After I retired, I had a couple of years coaching the Victoriaville Tigers in junior hockey. I currently do some public relations work for the Buffalo Sabres.

JEAN RATELLE

Jean Ratelle, after taking almost five seasons to make it to the NHL, went on to become the sixth leading scorer in league history by the time he retired in 1981. He spent 15 seasons with the New York Rangers, many of them as a member of the GAG (goal a game) line flanked by Rod Gilbert and Vic Hadfield. He was a major part of the 1975 deal that brought Phil Esposito to New York with Carol Vadnais. In return, he and Brad Park and a minor leaguer went to Boston. Ratelle, known for his stylish behavior on and off the ice, played in 21 seasons, scoring 491 goals and 1,267 points.

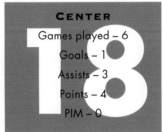

CENTER
18
Games played – 6
Goals – 1
Assists – 3
Points – 4
PIM – 0

It lasted only a month, but playing on Team Canada in '72 will always be a special part of my life in hockey – a real highlight. And the friends I made on that team will always be very special.

My best memory, I think, was coming back from that big deficit, that hole we were in, and winning the last three games in Moscow. That was unforgettable. By then we were in top shape, and had all of our lines clicking together, so we were able to play with much more confidence. We knew by then that we had a good chance of winning the series, despite getting off to such a bad start in Canada.

I played in the games in Toronto and Winnipeg – games two and three – and all four games in Moscow. It was a privilege to get so much ice time because there were so many talented players on our team. I think our defensemen – all of them – played superbly in Moscow and deserve a lot of credit for our wins over there. I was particularly impressed with the performance of Gary Bergman.

I remember in one game Bergman tangled with Mikhailov behind the net and they had their arms wrapped around each other. Then Mikhailov kicked Bergman in the shins a couple of times. Hard kicks. Bergman was so mad he banged the Russian player's head into the wire mesh. Most of us had never seen one player kicking an opponent with his skates. It just didn't happen in the NHL and there was almost a big brawl when Mikhailov did that.

Jean Ratelle at the Hockey Hall of Fame.

I was glad I stayed because I got to play with one of the greatest guys I've ever met – Jean Ratelle. He reminded me of Jean Beliveau – classy. He was very good to play with, very encouraging. I played with him in Vancouver, where he told me, "Just relax and play your own game." – *Dennis Hull*

Ratelle tries to break past a persistent Gennady Tsigankov as Anatoli Firsov rushes toward the action.

Among the forwards, Paul Henderson excelled, of course, with his winning goals. And Phil Esposito, who played the best hockey of his life, provided us with great leadership.

It was a great experience going to Russia to play hockey. It showed us a different way of life and while none of us would want to live over there, it gave us an insight into a different kind of culture.

And to our surprise we found out all too quickly that the Russian players had all the necessary skills to play the game at the highest level. There wasn't what you might call a "second rate" player among them. They were all of NHL caliber in my opinion. Yakushev was a great winger and Tretiak was outstanding in goal. Kharlamov and Mikhailov were also very good. What impressed me about them was that they were very, very strong. Not too big, perhaps, but very strong. I'm sure it was because of the way they trained, with land training and soccer and working out 11 months of the year. They played a different style of hockey, with behind-the-back passes — lots of passes. It took us awhile to adjust and it took our very best effort to beat them.

I retired from the Bruins in 1980–81 and since then I've remained active in hockey. I was assistant coach to Gerry Cheevers for four years when he coached the Bruins. In 1985–86, I became a scout for the Bruins, mostly working in the United States. For the last five or six years I've been scouting in the east, mostly at the college level in the New England area. I've seen a lot of college players move into the NHL in the past few years. A few months ago I decided to retire from the game permanently. But I know the game I loved to play will always be a part of me.

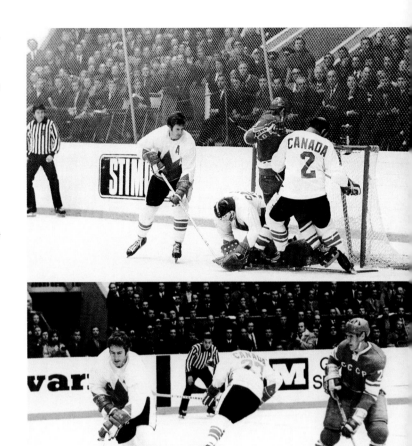

Top: Ken Dryden stops the puck with some help from Ratelle and Gary Bergman; middle: Ratelle gains control of the puck; bottom: Ratelle has a shadow as he attempts to get the puck to the net.

Then, in the final seconds, Henderson's dramatic goal. He wasn't even supposed to have been on the ice in those critical seconds. Neither was Esposito perhaps, because he was at the end of a long shift. He would say later, "There was no way I was going off. It's gonna happen and I want to be part of it when it does."
– *Ken Dryden*

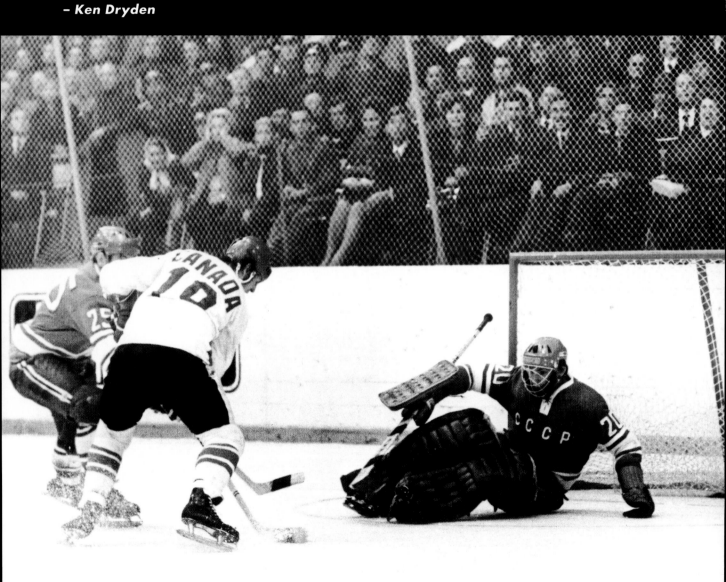

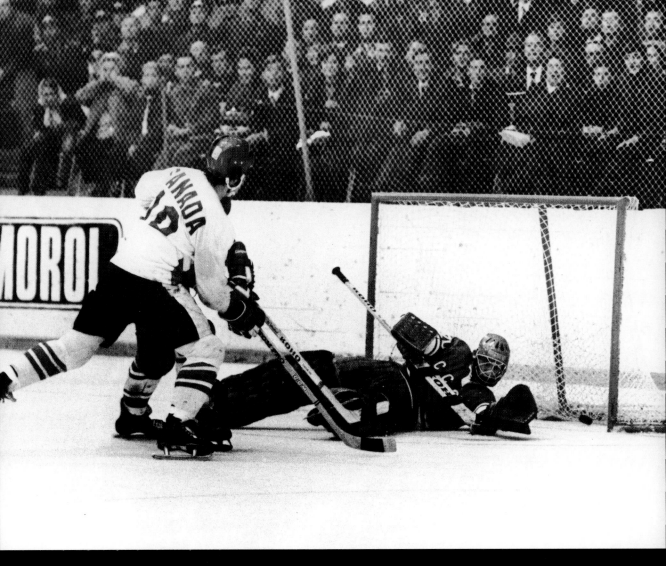

Then came Henderson's heroics and the game-winning goal. I can't understand why Tretiak didn't stop Henderson's shot. Paul came out in front – he was so alone there – and simply banged away at it and it went in. – *Dennis Hull*

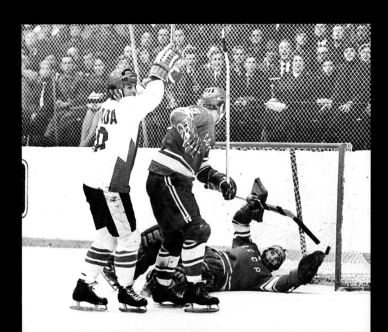

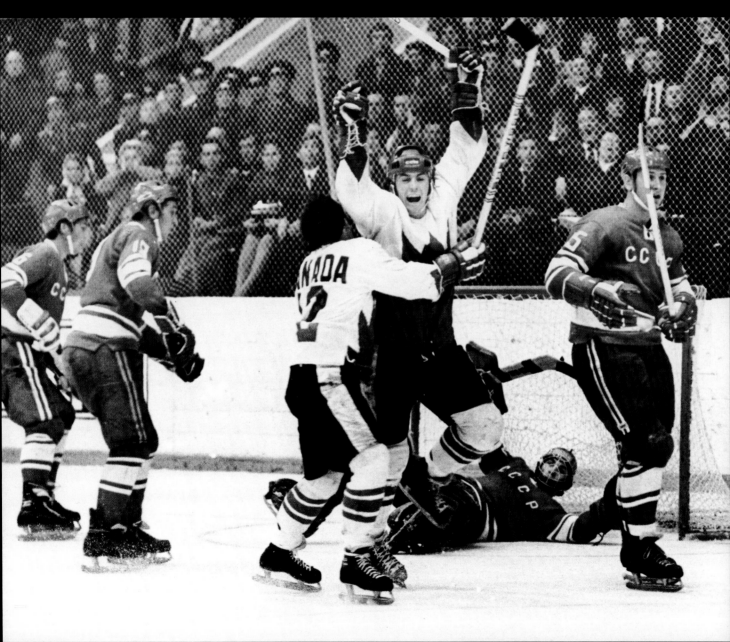

The best moment of the series, the one that I really enjoy remembering, is when Henderson scored the winning goal in the last game. The relief of that was unbelievable.
– Brad Park

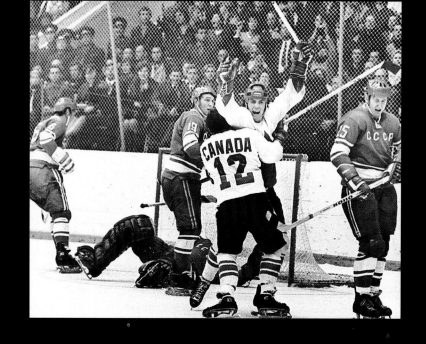

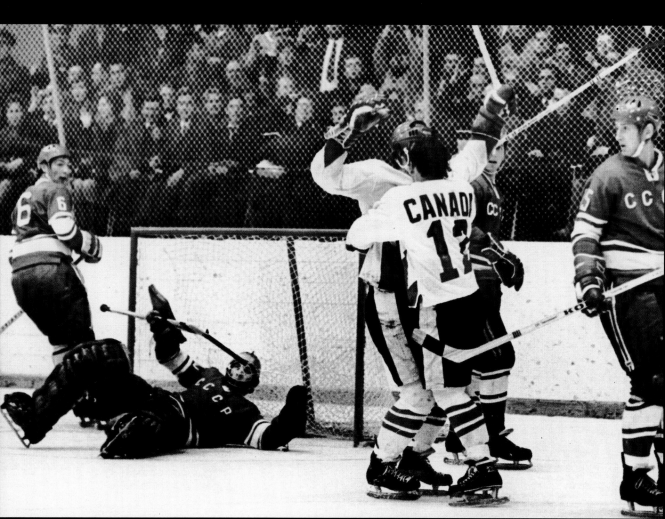

When Paul Henderson jumped in my arms and said, "We did it! We did it!" – that was the very highest point of the series. We knew the expectations of the Canadian people. It was to win. We *had* to win. – *Yvan Cournoyer*

I think that our pride and determination helped us a lot, especially in that final game. It was such an emotional win. I have never seen grown men cry like our guys did. We were all overcome, all exhausted, all just overjoyed. – *Ed Johnston*

MICKEY REDMOND

Mickey Redmond was the first player in Detroit history to score 50 goals, scoring 52 in 1972–73. He was a member of two Stanley Cup winning teams (Montreal) in his first two seasons, then was traded to Detroit (for Frank Mahovlich) on January 13, 1971. He played in nine seasons and 538 games before injuries terminated his career. He finished with 233 goals and 428 points.

In '76, four years after our victory in Moscow, I retired from the game because of back surgery and other health problems that prohibited me from skating like I once did. Since then I have been involved in television work; for *Hockey Night in Canada* for five years, and then with ESPN for several years, and now full time with the Detroit Red Wings, my former club. So I am fortunate to be close to the game we all grew up to love. It really is a full-time job for me. We broadcast a full schedule of 82 games and it keeps me pretty busy, with 30 teams in the league and all the travel involved.

We've had a couple of good years in Detroit recently, with the two Stanley Cups. We got a bit spoiled in 1997 and 1998 and went almost until the first of July with the Cup wins and all the festivities that

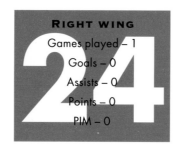

RIGHT WING
Games played – 1
Goals – 0
Assists – 0
Points – 0
PIM – 0
24

followed them. Then for the Red Wings to get beat out in the first round in 2001 brought the longest stretch I've been off work for about 10 years. It's a strange feeling not to be around hockey for four and a half months.

I think the best memory I have of '72 would be the remarkable comeback. Through poor scouting and misinformation, we were unprepared going into that series, not realizing what skilled players we were up against, and it took us awhile to get our bearings. Two things really jump out at me. First, it was the ability of Team Canada '72 to quickly adjust to a great hockey team, and a system that the Soviets employed at the time, that allowed us to make that comeback. Second, to win those last three games all by one goal was remarkable. Those are the memories that come rushing back.

The feeling we got from representing Canada and having the support that we received basically across the board through letters, phone calls, the entire country stopping to watch games – well, for a hockey player, there is no greater feeling in the world.

On the non-hockey side, the best memory I have was that I took my mom with me. Peter Mahovlich and I both took our mothers and they roomed together and had an absolutely wonderful time over there. My dad had been overseas playing hockey during the war, and when the trip was brought up, he said, "Why don't you take your mother, because she's never been over there?" So I did and, by gosh, she had a wonderful time. I can still remember very fondly some of the fun we had and the enjoyment we got out of having our mothers around. I know she really enjoyed that. She and Mrs. Mahovlich together had a lot of fun trading and exchanging things like nylons and chocolate bars with the Russian people.

I don't regret anything about the adventure. I was chosen to play in the first game and then, of course, we lost that one by a big score. Naturally, they made lineup changes and I never got back in after that, and that was certainly disappointing. But having been chosen as one of probably the 40 best hockey players in the world, at least in our part of the world, that was a great feeling for me. Then I took sick when we were half way to Sweden and I got sick again in Czechoslovakia, so there were times I couldn't have played even if they had wanted me to.

But just being part of that whole experience – a first for a Canadian pro – was a tremendous thrill. The feeling we got from representing Canada and having the support that we received basically across the board through letters, phone calls, the entire country stopping to watch games – well, for a hockey player, there is no greater feeling in the world. So it became a huge thrill to be representing your country in the greatest series ever played.

There were a lot of players who contributed in a lot of different ways to our success. Paul Henderson was certainly in the right place at the right time and scored the big goals, but when you watch the games, a player like Jean-Paul Parise stood out – a guy who played for Minnesota for many years, just an up and down hard-working guy. There

Redmond at practice in training camp.

were guys like Ron Ellis and Bobby Clarke, Rod Seiling and Gary Bergman, they played really well. These guys were not all-star types, maybe Bobby Clarke was, but they contributed an awful lot to the victory. Of course Cournoyer and the Espositos, the Mahovlichs and Henderson were the star names that everybody knew, but there were a lot of guys who did a lot of outstanding work to help finally put the Soviets away.

The refereeing is a distant memory now, but I do recall it was pretty difficult for us to adapt to what

Mickey Redmond with the Detroit Red Wings.

just unbelievable to sit on the bench and watch him go. I think each of us who has played this game at the NHL level has, at one time or another, encountered somebody who he's played against that when he goes to the bench, no matter who he is, says, "Can you believe what a skilled player this guy is? What a great player."

Tretiak was much better than anyone believed he could be. And the Soviets' hockey system gave us some concern. They didn't shoot the puck when there was an opportunity, like we did, and they didn't go to the front of the net. And on a rush, they made two or three more passes than we normally did.

I think our system and our way of playing became difficult for Tretiak to adjust to. Although he was a great goaltender, he wasn't used to traffic in front of his net and screen plays and deflections and things like that. The way the Soviets played the game was to complete the perfect pass and the open net shot, and often it turned out to be a pass or two too many.

we felt were atrocious calls being made and obvious bias. Perhaps they felt the same thing on the other side, I don't know. It was just something we had to overcome and try to ignore. As difficult as it was, we were able to do it, and I guess if the squeaky wheel gets the grease, then I think we squeaked enough.

The Soviets were such a great hockey team. But I think the fellow who died in the car crash, Kharlamov, I don't know if I have ever seen a hockey player as skilled and agile as that man was. It was

There's no question they were a team that came in and surprised us. Everybody thought we were going to beat them eight straight games and wipe them out. But they were well skilled, well trained, well prepared — much more than we were.

Remember, we weren't accustomed to summertime hockey and we didn't work out as hard as we might have. Then to find out that we were up against a very formidable foe made it necessary to really bear down in very quick fashion. It showed the resilience of Canadian hockey players and what we could do with our minds even when our bodies weren't in sync. Somehow we found a way to do it and there was a great satisfaction in that.

I think our system and our way of playing became difficult for Tretiak to adjust to. Although he was a great goaltender, he wasn't used to traffic in front of his net and screen plays and deflections and things like that. The way the Soviets played the game was to complete the perfect pass and the open net shot, and often it turned out to be a pass or two too many.

SERGE SAVARD

Serge Savard, during 15 seasons on the Montreal blueline, held the Stanley Cup on eight occasions. He became the first defenseman to capture the Conn Smythe Trophy as playoff MVP in 1969. He also won the Bill Masterton Memorial Trophy in 1979. He was a key member of Montreal's Big Three and was at his best during Montreal's four consecutive Cup-winning seasons from 1976 to 1979. Savard retired in 1981 was but persuaded by his friend John Ferguson to join the Winnipeg Jets for a couple of seasons, after which he retired permanently. Later he served as general manager of the Habs and saw his teams win two more Cups, in 1986 and 1993.

The highlight of the series was of course the final goal by Paul Henderson. I can't begin to describe how filled with emotion we all were when we won that series. When we started out, it took awhile for us to come together as a team — after all, we had played for many years learning how to hate the opposing players in the NHL and suddenly you're sitting down next to Phil Esposito, or Bobby Clarke or Stan Mikita, and we're on the ice together all pulling together for one cause and all going in the same direction.

The fans were really pulling for us too, at least in the beginning. We were caught by surprise in Montreal. We didn't quite prepare for the series the way we possibly could have and it took us awhile to get going. I don't think we had the best team possible. It would have been nice to have Bobby Orr in the lineup, and other players like Bobby Hull. Orr would have made a tremendous difference in the series, I'm sure. I think the best Team Canada was put together in '76 when we won the Canada Cup.

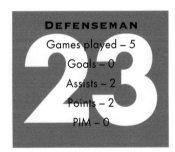

DEFENSEMAN
23
Games played – 5
Goals – 0
Assists – 2
Points – 2
PIM – 0

Two guys really impressed me in the series. Number one was Phil Esposito. Before the series, I didn't have that much respect for Phil. He played in Bobby Orr's shadow. When Orr was injured and unable to play, Esposito really came into his own, he unleashed so much talent. The other star, and one who was probably not in the same category as Phil, was Peter Mahovlich. I thought he played a tremendous role in the series.

I was very lucky to play in all the winning games in the series, but after the game in Winnipeg

The celebration begins: Team Canada celebrates a stunning victory.

My friend Serge Savard, in the morning workout in Vancouver, suffered a hairline fracture of his ankle after stopping a puck. Some people said he was through for the series. They didn't know Serge. He came back for game six in Moscow – not fully recovered from his ankle injury but still one of the best defensemen in hockey history. – *Guy Lapointe*

Aleksandr Yakushev aims a backhand shot at Ken Dryden while Savard and Guy Lapointe try to block the shot.

I thought my series was over. I suffered an injury and when I got to Vancouver, they found a hairline fracture in my leg. They took some tests and I flew back to Montreal and luckily had 10 days there to recuperate. I decided to continue playing in the series and go to Russia, and I got to play in the second game [game six] over there and finish the series in Moscow.

Kharlamov was the best of the Soviets in my opinion. I ended up playing against him in that famous New Year's Eve game in Montreal and he had all the moves.

John Ferguson was an excellent choice to help coach Harry Sinden behind the bench. There's a famous story about how we were all on a float in Montreal and we called Prime Minister Pierre

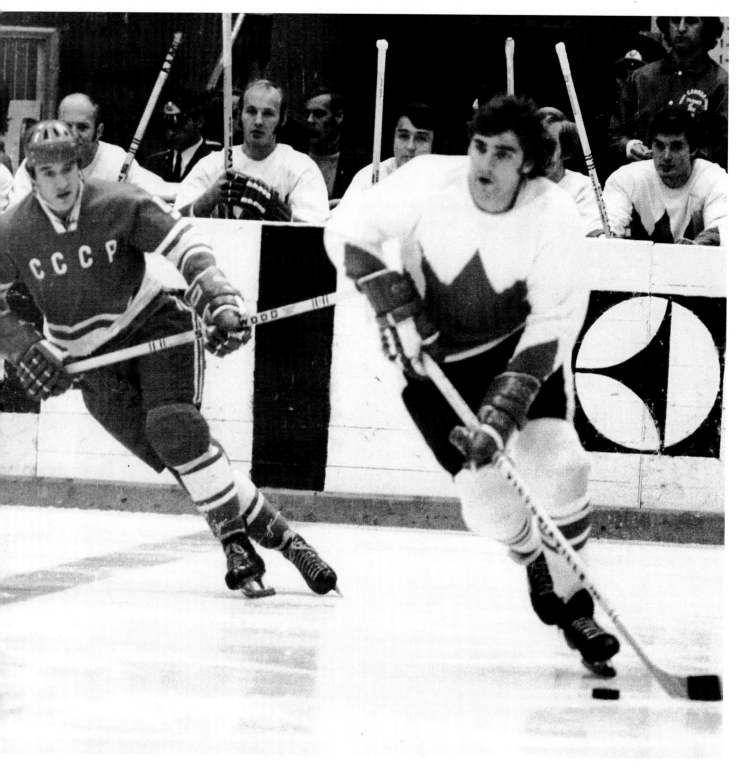

Savard whirls by the Team Canada bench in Moscow.

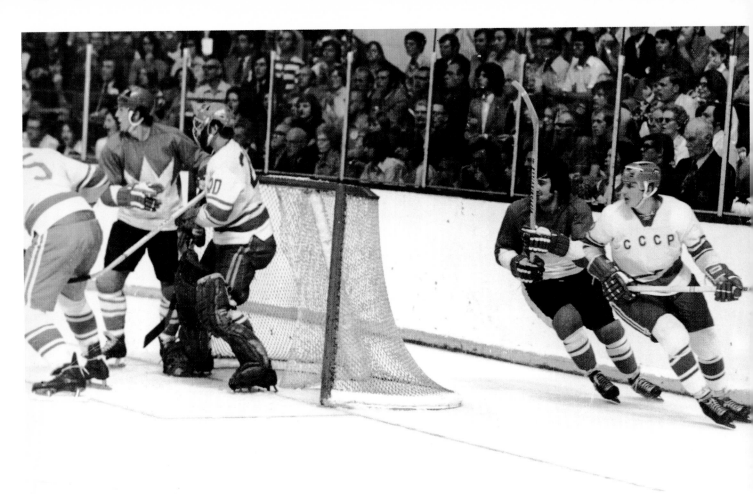

Savard, right, circles the Soviet net with his shadow, while Paul Henderson tries to insert himself between Aleksandr Ragulin and Vladislav Tretiak.

I persuaded Harry to take Serge Savard even though he had just come off a broken leg, but he was still one of the premier defensemen in the National League. He played in every game we won. – *John Ferguson*

Serge Savard at the Hocky Hall of Fame in 1997.

Trudeau aboard. I took Fergie's stick, signed by all the players, and gave it to the Prime Minister. I told him Fergie wanted him to have it. Fergie was fuming. When my little prank appeared as a story in the newspaper the next day, I believe Fergie got the stick back, but I'm not sure of that. Of course, Fergie always liked to return one practical joke with another. I remember one time in Winnipeg when my car windows were covered with Vaseline and Winnipeg Jets stickers. So when you played a joke on Fergie you knew you were going to get it back somewhere down the line.

All in all, playing on that great team in '72 was a wonderful experience. I had been on Stanley Cup teams but it was nothing quite like winning against the Soviets that year.

ROD SEILING

Rod Seiling began his NHL career with the Toronto Maple Leafs after playing junior hockey with the Toronto Marlboros and in the 1964 Olympics, where he scored six points in seven games. He was traded to New York on February 4, 1964, as part of a deal that brought Andy Bathgate to the Leafs. After 11 years on Broadway, he went back to the Leafs for two seasons, before being signed (as a free agent) by St. Louis in 1976. He was sold to Atlanta midway through the 1978–79 season, then retired. Seiling played in 979 games and collected 269 points.

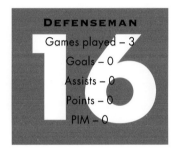

DEFENSEMAN
16
Games played – 3
Goals – 0
Assists – 0
Points – 0
PIM – 0

The best memory, obviously, was winning the series. That, and the friendships that I made along the way. The camaraderie that we established — it was like going to war together — was very special to us all. We formed friendships and bonds so strong that we'll have them for a lifetime. Then, of course, there was the winning, and in such an unexpected way. We left Canada for Sweden and Russia with only our friends and relatives, and maybe not even those, promising their support. When we left, we knew people thought we had let them down. They all expected an easy, one-sided victory, especially in the games in Canada, and leaving after four games played with only one win and a tie was a real downer. And the prospects of not doing any better, perhaps doing even worse, in Russia left most Canadians with a sour taste in their mouths about Team Canada.

In Sweden, where we played a couple of exhibition games, even the Canadian ambassador to Sweden was not very kind to us and made references to the "ruffian team from Canada" in his comments at a reception he held for the team.

But when we got to Moscow, the 3,000 Canadians that traveled there to lend their support were fabulous. They did so much for us. Many of them got to see the walls in our dressing room, where every square inch was plastered with telegrams, all wishing us well. It was a wonderful boost to our morale. It gave us an indication that Canadians were supporting us after all, and that was very gratifying.

Seiling makes a grab for Vladimir Shadrin's puck, Guy Lapointe as backup.

Remember, those were the days of the Cold War. It was us against them; our way of life versus the communist way of life. And we came through, if only by the slimmest of margins.

A bad moment for Seiling at the Montreal game as the puck flies past him to Ken Dryden, with Peter Mahovlich out of reach.

Memories have a way of erasing negative thoughts and just focusing on the good things, so it was a good time, a good feeling and, of course, as the years slip by, it only gets better.

I remember how impressed I was with some of the Russians – players like Maltsev, Yakushev, Kharlamov and, of course, the goaltender Tretiak. I had played the Russians a few years earlier as a junior and had gained a great deal of respect for them. I was impressed with their ability to operate at peak proficiency, and, of course, for our series in '72, they were in mid-season form and we weren't. That was, at first, a major part of the problem. We simply weren't prepared and they were. Fortu-nately, we became much better conditioned as the series moved along, and I think we also under-stood a little better how to play against them. They cycled the puck a lot and we started the series playing a traditional NHL-style game, which we soon discovered didn't work very well against the Russians. So we regrouped, made some changes and we won.

For me, there was a great deal of self-satisfaction in being a member of a team representing Cana-da, a team that pulled itself together and, almost against all odds, wound up beating the Russians in very dramatic style. Remember, those were the

Seiling breaks for center ice, with Yvan Cournoyer ready in the wings.

days of the Cold War. It was us against them; our way of life versus the communist way of life. And we came through, if only by the slimmest of margins.

To this day, I'm amazed at how many people still remember me as a member of Team Canada. It's something that I live with, I'm comfortable with and something that makes me proud. It's nice to be remembered for being part of a series that came to mean so much to Canadians. Even young people seem to know about it. When we held a team reunion in Toronto last fall for the unveiling of the commemorative statue that the Canadian mint had designed for us, it was amazing to see the number of young people there. When you think about it, it's been 30 years. None of the kids there that day were even born when that series took place. Some of their parents hadn't been born. But they turned out for us. They stood out in the rain, they knew all the players, they knew what had happened. It was truly amazing.

I turned to business after hockey and I enjoy a good life. I'm currently president of the Greater Toronto Hotel Association. I've been in that posi-

tion for eight years now. Prior to that, I was in the horse racing industry with the Ontario Jockey Club. For a number of years I owned and operated my own horse breeding operation.

I learned that my life as a hockey player would help open doors to me. I also learned it's not much help if you don't know what to say or how to act when that door swings open. My career as a pro athlete taught me a lot about life, and about people, and certainly the Team Canada experience was a great plus for me.

Bill White and Rod Seiling, front, at a Team Canada reunion.

HARRY SINDEN

Harry Sinden has served as general manager of the Boston Bruins (1972–73) and as president of the Bruins (1989–90). He was the first NHL general manager to be involved in 1,000 wins. An amateur star in senior hockey, Sinden led the Whitby Dunlops to the Allan Cup championship in 1957 and 1959. He also led the Dunnies to the World title in 1958 and played for Kitchener's silver-medal-winning team in the 1960 Winter Olympics. He joined Boston as head coach in the 1966–67 season and guided the Bruins to the Stanley Cup in 1970, their first Cup triumph in 29 years. He entered private business following the Cup celebration in 1970, joined Team Canada in 1972 and rejoined the Bruins as general manager for 1972–73. He was elected to the Hockey Hall of Fame as a builder in 1983.

HEAD COACH

Probably the first high moment of the series for me – and for Team Canada – was Peter Mahovlich's shorthanded goal in Toronto in game two. Coming off the very lowest moment, the bitterness and humiliation we suffered in Montreal in game one, that spectacular goal by Pete helped us to a victory at Maple Leaf Gardens. It was a goal I'll never forget, an uplifting moment for the team in a game we urgently needed to win.

Another satisfying moment for me as coach came after the first game we played in Moscow, even though we lost the match. Every player on Team Canada knew it was the best game we had played to

that point. It looked like we were every bit as good as the Russians were – perhaps even a little bit better – so that gave us a lift even though we lost.

That game followed by a few days the absolute lowest moment in the series – the defeat we suffered in Vancouver. That loss was a shocker because we seemed to lose not only our poise, which was discouraging, but we also seemed to lose our fans. And that was a real blow to me and the players.

After the Vancouver loss, I knew Phil Esposito was out there on the ice giving an interview on television. But I had no idea it was such an emotional speech. I didn't get to hear it until I got back to the hotel and watched it on TV with John Ferguson. And I was very touched. I was moved by it like I think most Canadians were. Phil was just dripping with sincerity – and perspiration. I think all the players saw it like Fergie and I did, and I think Phil's honest, straightforward appeal contributed greatly to us not losing faith. Fortunately we had a week in Sweden to regroup, to get ourselves together and forget the Vancouver debacle,

With all the star players I had to work with – and there were many – putting lines together was a bit of a lottery. The truth be known, most of the time you luck out or you don't. In the case of the Clarke-Henderson-Ellis line, I really did luck out because, frankly, I didn't know where to go with Bobby Clarke. He was just a kid and he ended up centering those two.

but that performance was a pretty low point in our hockey lives, there's no doubt.

With all the star players I had to work with — and there were many — putting lines together was a bit of a lottery. When they are successful at forming lines, coaches like to say, "You know, I saw this strength in one player and this quality in another, and this skill in a third and I thought they would make a balanced line so I put them together." The truth be known, most of the time you luck out or you don't. In the case of the Clarke-Henderson-Ellis line, I really did luck out because, frankly, I didn't know where to go with Bobby Clarke. He was just a kid and he ended up centering those two. We didn't really know the offensive strength of Bobby Clarke at that time but it turned out he had everything we wanted. I can see why Ellis and Henderson might have wanted somebody like Esposito or Ratelle to center them as opposed to Clarke. But the line became so successful because there was a real balance there. On right wing, Ronnie Ellis was such a tremendous all-round player. I especially admired his strength defensively. And Paul Henderson, on left wing, scored all those big goals. From day one, it was a line with a balance that was almost magical.

Paul Henderson was one of the highlights. He and Phil Esposito were two players that you could pick out of all the players in that series and give them five stars. At that time, I don't think Paul's Christian beliefs were as strong as they are today, although most of us I suppose were good Christians. But he was the guy who scored the goal of the century, the guy who scored the most goals of anybody in the series, and to have him front and center representing that team in admirable fashion since the end of the series has been another slice of good fortune for that entire group.

John Ferguson, left, and Sinden at training camp in Toronto.

I loved working with John Ferguson. He passed up an opportunity to play for Team Canada that year. And I'm glad he stuck to coaching. He was invaluable and gave a lot of input and balance to the coaching staff. When I had a particularly sensitive problem with some of the players he was able to put things in perspective — to speak the same language as them. I know they all respected him and that helped me a lot.

Sinden

179

The thrills, the turmoil, the passion, the stunning surprises of that rollercoaster ride in '72 caused our emotions to run wild, not only among the players in the locker rooms and on the ice, in the hotels and on the airplanes, but also among the fans who alternately supported us and critiqued us. And in the end, they roared their approval of us and loved us when we came home. Those feelings have never gone away.

Harry Sinden at the Hockey Hall of Fame.

As for those players who grew frustrated and decided to leave the team in Moscow, I don't think there was a lot of anger or resentment toward them. It was like, "Well, that's the way they want it. If they leave, we'll just carry on." It was that kind of approach. The ones who stayed said, "Well, we're here. This is a challenge. We'll do what we have to do." A couple who left us — like Perreault and Martin — were quite young and perhaps felt, rightfully, that their chances of playing a lot in Moscow were rather slim.

I'd like to single out the late Gary Bergman as an unsung hero who produced a lot and surprised me. He probably played the best eight games of his life in the series and he was as steady as a rock on our defense. Bill White was another one we could

always count on. We had six defensemen there and as the series evolved it turned out those six were playing all the time. And no matter which pair it was, other than on the power play, you didn't have to pick and choose who went out there to stop those speedy Russian forwards. That's because Bergman, White, Stapleton, Park, Savard and Lapointe all came armed with tremendous credentials from the NHL. At least half of our defensemen had Hall of Fame potential — Park, Savard and Lapointe were certainties even at that time. White and Bergman may not have been quite in that class in terms of what we knew about them, but suddenly we had two guys who could play every bit as well as the ones we knew were great players. That really bolstered our team, the fact that those two were able to hold up their end as well as they did.

The refereeing over there was atrocious. There was always a lot going on behind the scenes to make us suspicious. We found out later that everything we try to guard against in this country in terms of officials — by that I mean bribery or attempting to influence the officials in any way — was rampant over there.

Before the final game, the official who was supposed to referee, a Swedish fellow, bowed out. They told us he was sick and couldn't make it, and that the East German referee was going to handle the game. That's the kind of thing that rattled us. John Ferguson became so upset, so furious with the change, that he threatened not to play the game. When we tried to reason with Fergie, he said, "You'll have to go through me." And he was talking to us, his own people. He was so livid over the fact that they were manipulating the refereeing that at an emergency meeting, Ferguson said flat out, "We're not playing." I recall saying to him, "Now, wait a minute, Johnnie…" and he turned on me and all the officials and shouted, "What do you mean, wait a minute? If I say we're not playing, we're not playing." That raised a few eyebrows. And I smile today when I recall his outburst. We all know Fergie has a physical presence that can be intimidating. That day he had a physical manner in his speech. I hate to think what might have happened if one of the group had challenged him.

I'm sure our goaltenders, Ken Dryden and Tony Esposito, have some strong memories — both good and bad — of that series. They were two of the finest netminders in the world but neither of them had ever played against a team like that. I give a lot of credit to that Soviet club. That was a fantastic team, one of the greatest I've ever seen, and every bit as good as we were. Their style of play, the size of the ice surface in Moscow they played on, probably contributed largely to their success. Most of the shots they took had a good chance of going in the net. If they didn't, they simply wouldn't take the shot. Our goalies expected shots that never came, and it took some adjusting. And in my opinion, for whatever reason, I really don't think that either Ken or Tony played up to the form they had consistently displayed in the NHL. I don't mean to imply that they were really off form or really bad, but facing facts, the Russians had the outstanding goaltending and we didn't.

Tretiak's superb goaltending greatly surprised me. We didn't know anything about him until we received a scouting report stating that he wasn't very good. Our scouts went over there to look at his team in action and Tretiak let in eight goals or something like that. The scouts came back and said the Russian goaltending was lousy. Well, it turns out Tretiak got married that afternoon, or maybe it was the night before, and that may have thrown him off his usual solid performance. But wasn't he

Tony Esposito and Vladislav Tretiak shake, with Phil Esposito and Johnny Esau looking on.

fantastic against us? And only 20 years old. Tretiak, Henderson and Yakushev, and Kharlamov and Esposito were the really top players.

So many years have passed since that September in '72, and most of us getting along in years have memories of that great series that shine like polished silver. I like to describe the event like a really fine wine, one you savor and recall decades later. The taste just never goes away.

The thrills, the turmoil, the passion, the stunning surprises of that rollercoaster ride in '72 caused our emotions to run wild, not only among the players in the locker rooms and on the ice, in the hotels and on the airplanes, but also among the fans who alternately supported us and critiqued us. And in the end, they roared their approval of us and loved us when we came home. Those feelings have never gone away.

Looking back, I can recall almost everything that happened on each and every day during that time, from the shocking setback in Montreal to the riveting final seconds in Moscow. Some of the moments are clouded, but no other event in my entire life can I remember as clearly, and as fondly, as that one.

PAT STAPLETON

Pat Stapleton was claimed by Boston from Chicago in the 1961 intra-league draft and was dealt to Toronto in 1965. Before he could play a game for the Leafs, he was reclaimed by Chicago in the intra-league draft of 1965 and played solid hockey for the Blackhawks until 1973, when he jumped to the Chicago Cougars of the WHA. He played another five years in the upstart league – for a time as part owner of the team – before retiring in 1978.

I don't have any bad memories of Team Canada in 1972. There were a lot of things that you could mull over and decide that they were learning curves, but I can honestly say there is not a bad memory. It was certainly a learning experience for all of us.

They say I was one of the guys who pulled off a lot of gags in Moscow. Well, that's always important to a team, keeping things light. There was enough stress and enough pressure being placed on us by outside sources. The expectations were so high; having a little fun breaks the tension. Actually, now that I think back on it, I have to blame Bill White for those gags I mentioned. I had very little to do with them. And somebody has to take the blame.

The deal that I think was funniest was the time everybody got on the bus that was booked to go to a Chinese restaurant. One day Bill White and I were standing around and somebody said, "Where have you guys been?" We said, "Oh, we just got back from a great Chinese restaurant." I think we even had a name for it – the Pe King if I remember right. There was a game the next day and then

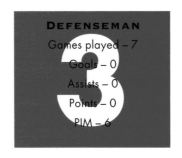

DEFENSEMAN
Games played – 7
Goals – 0
Assists – 0
Points – 0
PIM – 6

after that everybody wanted to go for Chinese food because they were fed up with the food that they were getting. They thought that a nice Chinese dinner would be great. So they all agreed to go, and Bill and I helped out by ordering a bus. Everybody showed up and got on the bus. But Bill and I didn't show.

As for the players involved, from the Canadian side, I was certainly impressed with everyone selected. Their determination to come back and win, against all the odds, was a tremendous feat. It could only have happened on a team with grit and guts like that one.

We went into a situation where we were led to believe that our players were superior because of our presence and stature in the National Hockey League. We were told we were top caliber – the best. But we soon realized that on the playing field you should never underestimate your opponent and never believe your press clippings. In that first game in Montreal, it was like we were thrust into the seventh game of the Stanley Cup Finals. And we weren't ready for that kind of pace.

I think a major factor in our success was the Russians' inability to vary from their strategy. They had a set offensive and defensive strategy and it never altered very much. They weren't individually creative. Once you learned what they were going to do and how they were going to do it, you could defend against it.

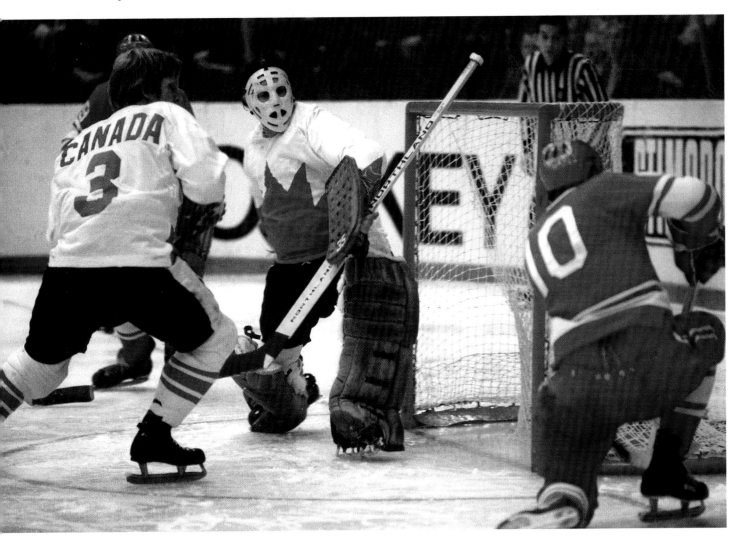

What impressed me, though, was the rallying ability of all the Team Canada guys. You could go down the list and every guy contributed all the skills he could muster, great spirit and attitude to develop a team concept. Even in the darkest days, after leaving Canada upset and frustrated, each individual played a part in staving off defeat. Certainly there were important moments, like Phil's speech in Vancouver, which I didn't get to hear until later. It was a defining moment and a rallying point for the Canadian fans. But in the privacy of our dressing room, everybody felt good about themselves — we wouldn't allow ourselves to get down, and we could still go ahead and play with confidence. The timing wasn't there at first. It was just a matter of being off by half a stride. The fierce competitive nature of the guys would come through in the end.

Pat Stapleton and Bill White played superbly in Moscow. When people talk about defensemen they talk about individuals – Bobby Orr, Brad Park, Ray Bourque. But working as a pair, there was nobody better than White and Stapleton in Moscow in '72. – *Dennis Hull*

Stapleton ties up Valeri Kharlamov before a watchful Tony Esposito and ever-ready Bill White.

I think a major factor in our success was the Russians' inability to vary from their strategy. They had a set offensive and defensive strategy and it never altered very much. They weren't individually creative. Once you learned what they were going to do and how they were going to do it, you could defend against it. I really enjoyed competing against them because it brought out the best in me, whether I was challenged by Yakushev or Petrov or Kharlamov. Bring 'em on. Their defensive guys were very good. They were great athletes to compete against. It was a fun time. There's not much need to say any more than that.

I think the impact of that series is still with us, still felt today. No matter where I go, people don't talk to me about what's happening in the NHL. They talk to me about what happened in that series in '72. Now as we all grow older, there are fewer and fewer people who remember it or were part of it, but I know the impact is there. A school year doesn't go by that I don't get calls to help with a project some young student is working on with a Team Canada theme. It's part of their research on Canadian history. They call and they talk about it. And not just kids. Just today I got a call from a guy who is 70 years old and still doing something on it. So that's the impact.

They all ask if I still have the puck that Henderson scored with, and that subject has created quite a little stir. If there's one specific thing they remember me for, I guess that's it. Everybody talks about that puck. I haven't decided yet how to give an answer. I mean, it's just a puck. What's a puck? It's three inches in diameter and one inch thick and it's black and it's rubber. And that puck is somewhere. Why all the fuss over a rubber puck? And that's my answer.

Thinking back, 30 years have skipped by pretty quick, haven't they? I don't know why but they seem to have flown by. When I retired from hockey after 15 years in the NHL and the WHA we came back home. I farmed up until a few years ago, then Jackie and I retired from the farm. We moved into Strathroy and we rented a home there. I have been assisting my son Tom, who has been in Sweden for the last 15 years. He brought over some heavy wash equipment for washing road trucks and we have established a R&D station in Sarnia which works on that equipment. Also, the system helps purify the dirty wash water and brings it back almost to its original state. That's kind of leading-edge stuff. Scandinavia is certainly ahead of Canada in that respect. It's been an interesting project over the last decade.

I also support our local junior B team here; both Jackie and I have been involved in that. We have supported them from the standpoint of raising the funds for young kids to play, and I've been involved in the coaching and the managing or the scouting – whatever it takes to make it happen. That is my bond with the game, and we still have a son, Mike, who plays the game professionally. In the pro game today it doesn't seem like you stay in one place very long. I believe hockey is more competitive now because you've got more countries

and more young people, men and women, wanting to play at the highest level.

Pat Stapleton with Ken Dryden.

I was part owner of a pro team once – the Chicago Cougars in the WHA. When the owners there decided that they were not going to continue, Ralph Backstrom, Dave Dryden and I – and a couple of others – pitched in and kept the club going for the rest of the year. It was a great experience. I certainly enjoyed it, but then I haven't done anything in my life that I haven't enjoyed. I was drinking tea out of my Peter Puck mug this morning and thinking it's important to tell people the fascinating history of our game. Peter was good at that, ahead of his time and he should be part of the game again. He could tell stories about Team Canada.

I see talented kids every day who I encourage to reach for the top. Many have the ability and if they are willing to put in the time and the hard work that brings success, they can do it.

DALE TALLON

Dale Tallon was Vancouver's first choice, second overall, in the 1970 Amateur Draft. He was second only to Gilbert Perreault, who was selected number one by Buffalo. After three seasons as a Canuck, Tallon was traded to Chicago, where he spent the next five years. Claimed by Pittsburgh, he played two more seasons before retiring in 1980. He was a long-time broadcaster of Blackhawks games and now serves the Hawks as director of player personnel.

My best memories of Team Canada are a combination of things, starting with the training camp in Toronto. That was a lot of fun. Then having an opportunity to witness the ups and downs in the first series in Canada and the emotional highs and lows of it all – that was

DEFENSEMAN
Games played – 0
32

memorable. At first I was on the roster as a forward but when we went to Sweden, I practiced and played both exhibition games on defense. I played very well and was told I was going to play in the first game in Russia, so I was really excited about that. Then, for political reasons I never quite understood, I never got to play. After that, I was told I'd be playing in the final game because of injuries to Bill White and Pat Stapleton. I suppose I was more nervous than I was excited that day. I skated in the warm-up, thinking I was going to play in the most important game in the history of hockey. Then both Stapleton and White announced that they were able to play. Sure I was let down and very disappointed.

Even though I didn't get to play in any of the meaningful games, I think the overall experience was exciting and a whole lot of fun. I remember sitting in Bobby Clarke's seat in the dressing room during the third period of the last game, hoping it was a lucky spot to sit – I knew he had a rabbit's foot hanging there somewhere. I didn't dare go out to watch after the second period. I just sat in the

Tallon embraces Russian fashion.

I remember sitting in Bobby Clarke's seat in the dressing room during the third period of the last game, hoping it was a lucky spot to sit – I knew he had a rabbit's foot hanging there somewhere. The tension in that period was almost unbearable.

room and listened for crowd reactions. I'd jump up and sneak out for a quick look and run back into the room again. The tension in that third period was almost unbearable.

Just the overall experience of playing with that group of great players and great people was a remarkable experience for me.

On our team, I remember how impressed I was when Phil took the stand in Vancouver. He stood up to the whole country and defended the team. That was impressive, especially for me, having been a player for the Canucks. Seeing and hearing the reaction from the fans there was unbelievable. We all knew Phil could score prior to that – he was a prolific scorer – but his overall play proved to me and everyone else that he was a great player.

The intensity level that Clarkie [Bobby Clarke] brought to the team was incredible too. And the role players were really phenomenal – players like J.P. Parise and Dennis Hull – it was amazing how quickly we became a team. That was the wonderful thing about it. Even if you weren't playing, the closeness of this group – still today – is really

indescribable. What these guys feel for each other is incredible.

Some of those Russian players deserve a lot of praise. That Kharlamov was phenomenal. I don't think that any of us had seen anybody who was as quick and as skilled as he was. It was almost like his skates never touched the ice.

For me, it's been the highlight of my career. I came back from Team Canada with the highest expectations. Everybody on the Canucks was positive. My problem was that no one knew where I should play – forward or defense. After Team Canada, it was pretty well set in my mind that I could play defense and play it well.

When you go out on a high like that and play on a team like Team Canada, then come back to a team like the one that really struggled in Vancouver – I think my expectations changed. I think I set bigger goals for myself and thought more about how things should be done. There were some disappointments after Team Canada, but overall it was a phenomenal trip for me. It makes me feel really proud to have played on that team.

After I retired, I became a broadcaster. I was a color commentator and analyst with the Blackhawks for 15 years. I've been in the golf business, too. I'm the head professional at the Highland Park Country Club. Now I'm working with the Blackhawks as the director of player personnel.

Dale Tallon at the Royal York Hotel, Toronto.

BILL WHITE

Bill White was a star defenseman in the American Hockey League with Rochester and Springfield for seven seasons before league expansion brought him to the L.A. Kings in 1967–68. He scored 11 goals in his rookie season there. White excelled with the Kings and was named to six all-star teams. On February 20, 1970, he was traded to Chicago, where he turned in six more excellent seasons. When injuries forced him out of the 1976–77 season he retired and began coaching junior hockey in Oshawa.

DEFENSEMAN

Games played – 7

Goals – 1

Assists – 1

Points – 1

PIM – 8

17

I'll never forget the last minute of that eighth game in Moscow. The highlight came when Paul Henderson rapped in the "goal of the century" against Tretiak. And I must say I was thrilled to be on the ice when that happened. We all leaped on Paul to celebrate what appeared to be the winning goal. And it did turn out to be the winner. But remember! There was still time for the Russians to come back and tie it up. We all cheered Henny's goal but we had to collect ourselves and kill off the final 34 seconds of the game. It may not sound like much, but 34 seconds can be an eternity in hockey, especially against the Soviets because they had such an explosive team.

In the final few seconds, a play came inside our blueline and I grabbed the puck and lofted it down the ice. Anything to get it out of our zone. I held my breath watching it because I was worried about an icing call. That would have brought the faceoff back deep into our zone, but one of their players skated fast enough to catch up to the puck and there was no whistle. Oh, I was relieved when that happened. It killed off a few more seconds and suddenly the game was over.

There was a really low point for me in that same game. Late in the second period, a Soviet player shot the puck hard for their fifth goal. I don't think you can see it on the video but it hit my knee and skipped past Kenny Dryden. I felt just awful. That made it 5–3 for the Soviets. A two-goal lead for them was a huge deficit for us to overcome. I was really down in the dumps when we went to the dressing room. That goal offset one I scored earlier in the game — my only goal of the series. Rod Gilbert fed me the puck as I raced in and I somehow threw it in the net behind Tretiak.

I always thought the Soviets tried a fix of some kind with the referees for the final game in Moscow. A Swedish referee had been assigned to the game but somehow he was pushed aside and the notorious Josef Kompalla, an East German ref, replaced him. I remember we threatened not to play because Kompalla was so biased against us. But we finally gave in and took to the ice.

Patty Stapleton provided much of the humor during the series. One night in Moscow between

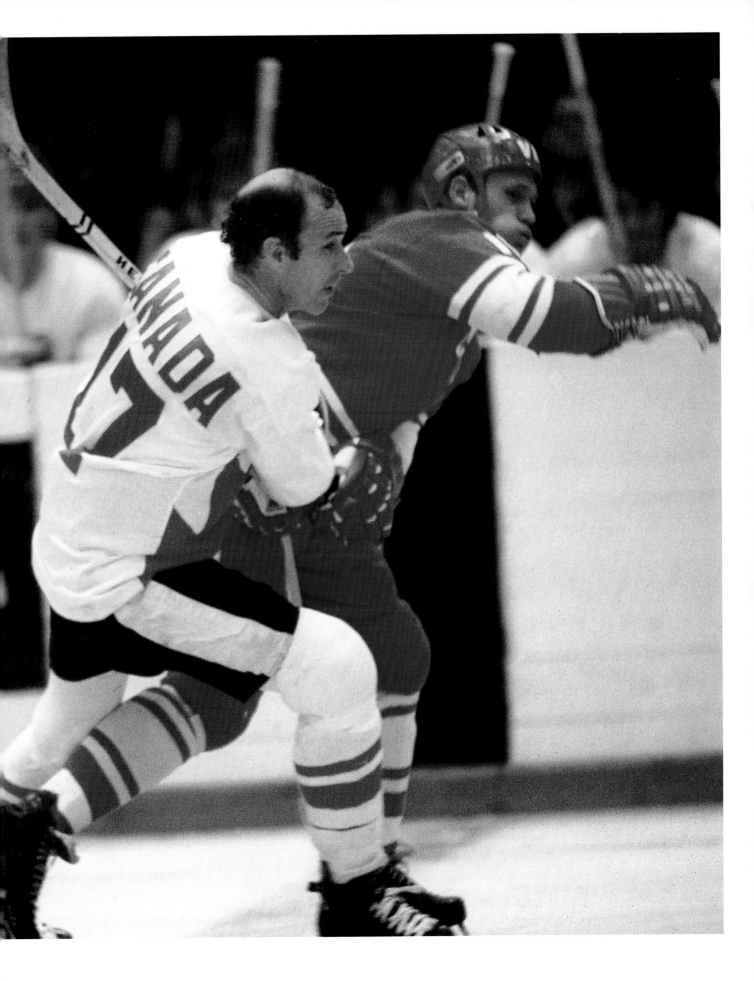

White outwits Vladislav Tretiak and forward Evgeni Mishakov to score a second-period goal in game eight.
Bottom: White assists Tony Esposito in stopping a Russian attack.

games he made everybody believe there was a
Chinese restaurant a couple of blocks away. He
had everybody anxious to go. And most of the
guys and their wives fell for it. He even arranged
for the team bus to pick them up and take them
there. Of course we didn't show up. And there was
no Chinese restaurant in all of Russia. But there
were 10 or 12 guys who went looking for it.

Pat and I had about six sticks autographed by all
the players, and we asked one of the team doctors
if he would look after them for us. But during the
flight back home, we took his blazer and used a

On the Soviet team, I liked Maltsev, number 10. He was a very crafty, very intelligent player who didn't waste any moves. He earned my utmost respect.

Adversaries on ice: White duels off with Aleksandr Maltsev to prevent him from getting the puck close to the Canadian net.

scalpel on the arms and down the back. There was just enough stitching left to hold it together. When the doctor got off the plane to meet the prime minister, he reached out to shake hands and the arm of his jacket fell right off. We never saw those sticks again.

People often ask me if Pat Stapleton has the puck from that game, the one Henderson scored with. Sure he does. I saw Pat pick up the puck. Oh yeah, he's got it. He just won't admit it. He skated around the net, and he was carrying the puck, and if you watch, as soon as the buzzer went, he reached down and picked it up. His father was a

great collector, too. He's got a lot of baseball rookie cards and stuff like that so it must be in his blood.

On Team Canada we were fortunate to have the leadership of Phil Esposito. He stood out among the 35 players chosen as the guy we looked to for the big play, the one who provided the inspiration. Of course, we all admired him for the way he came to bat for us after the loss in Vancouver. On the Soviet team, I liked Maltsev, number 10. He was a very crafty, very intelligent player who didn't waste any moves. He earned my utmost respect.

White becomes a human barrier, blocking a potentially deadly Russian shot. Below: Bill White relaxing with friends.

After the series I was a little disappointed because we were supposed to have a get-together with the Soviet players, but only three or four of them showed up. We were told all the others had come down with the flu. So we had our own party.

I carry the honor of being a Team Canada member with me to this day, three decades after the series. I'm in the plumbing wholesale business in Toronto. I've been involved in that for many years now — nothing too exciting. But no matter where I go, people seem to remember I was on that '72 team. And they say, "Wow! That must have been thrilling."

I wish everyone could have enjoyed the experience like I did. I'll never forget the fan support at home and in Moscow, all the telegrams we got from Canadians everywhere, all the best wishes. And the huge reception when we came home — first in Montreal and then in Toronto. We were all so happy to get back to Canada. It was unbelievable, simply fantastic.